TOUCHED BY THE JACKSONS

SPIRIT PUBLISHING™
A Division of Spirit Media
P.O. Box 43591
Phoenix, AZ 85080
**PROMOTIONAL COPY
NOT FOR SALE**
by Phoenix

TOUCHED BY THE JACKSONS

by Phoenix

SPIRIT PUBLISHING
PHOENIX, ARIZONA

Book Cover: Copyright © 1998 Arthur T. Phoenix

Front Cover Artwork
Designed and Created by: Arthur T. Phoenix
Illustrated by: Cesar Sanchez
Back Cover Photograph: **
Phoenix Rising poem written by: Arthur T. Phoenix © 1998
Book design and layout: Kubera Services, Prescott, Arizona

Published by **Spirit Publishing**, a division of **Spirit Media**
P.O. Box 43591
Phoenix, Arizona 85080

Copyright © 1998 by Arthur T. Phoenix. All rights reserved. Printed in the United States of America. No part of this publication may be reproduced or distributed in any form or by any means or stored in a data base or retrieval system without the prior written permission of both the copyright owner and the above publisher of this book.

Library of Congress Cataloging-in-Publication Data
Phoenix, Arthur T., 1964-
Touched By The Jacksons
1. Phoenix, Arthur T., 1964- . 2. Author- United States- Biography.
I. Title.

ISBN # 0-9663719-0-9
Library of Congress Catalog Card Number # 98-90321

First Edition

Photo Credits:
** — Arthur T. Phoenix
* — Weldon A. McDougal III

"This book is dedicated to the entire Jackson family:
Joseph, Katherine, Rebbie, Jackie, Tito, Jermaine, LaToya,
Marlon, Michael, Randy, and Janet."

"You made me what I am."

TOUCHED BY THE JACKSONS

Foreword

Behold the Mighty Jacksons in this compelling story about the world's most famous family in entertainment *history*: *the Jackson family*. This riveting book, written by Phoenix, a dedicated admirer for almost 30 years, will take you on a journey into the lives of the famous Jacksons, as he reveals the sacrifices, the sufferings, and the successes that the world's greatest entertainers endured throughout their illustrious careers. Learn how father, Joe Jackson, desperately seeking to remove his family from the industrial, inner-city life of Gary, Indiana, ruled his sons with an iron fist, trying to fulfill his lifelong dreams of fame and success through the lives of his sons. With enough blood, sweat, and determination, the Jackson brothers achieved the ultimate "American Dream" of success, ascending into the highest realm of fame and stardom. But along with fame comes the price you have to pay, as the Jacksons lived their lives through the press, surrounded by never-ending controversy. Phoenix discloses the details of brother Jermaine's departure from the group to pursue his solo career, the Jacksons' reunion on stage once again at the 1984 Victory Tour, sister LaToya's estrangement from her loving family, and the truth behind the molestation allegations against Michael and why he had to buy his way out of a diabolical scheme of extortion in order to clear his name. But unlike other books about the Jackson family, Phoenix recounts the facts directly from the most reliable sources: from his meetings with members of the Jackson family, their business associates, their personal friends, and other celebrities that have worked with them. The Jacksons' fame continues to endure, as they have sold a record breaking over 200 million records worldwide, and were inducted into the Rock and Roll Hall of Fame, symbolizing their legendary stature in music *history* throughout eternity.

Touched By The Jacksons, the gripping new book by Phoenix, will captivate and absorb you into the fascinating lives and careers of the Jacksons, making you feel as if you, too, have been *touched by the Jacksons*.

Table of Contents

The Legacy xi
Prelude xiii
Chapter 1: In The Beginning 1
Chapter 2: Bridge Over Troubled Water 9
Chapter 3: We're Here To Entertain You 19
Chapter 4: Jackson-mania!! 25
Chapter 5: Dancin' Machine 35
Chapter 6: Childhood 43
Chapter 7: Forever Came Today 49
Chapter 8: Destiny 55
Chapter 9: Goin' Places 61
Chapter 10: Girlfriend 65
Chapter 11: Triumph 73
Chapter 12: Forever Michael 81
Chapter 13: The King of Pop 89
Chapter 14: Human Nature 93
Chapter 15: Working Day and Night 99
Chapter 16: I Found That Girl 105
Chapter 17: Victory 107
Chapter 18: We Can Change The World 115
Chapter 19: Frontiers 119
Chapter 20: Gone Too Soon 123
Chapter 21: Never Can Say Goodbye 131
Chapter 22: Happy 135

Chapter 23: 2300 Jackson Street 143
Chapter 24: We've Got Forever 155
Chapter 25: The Dream Goes On 161
Chapter 26: Dangerous 169
Chapter 27: The Nightmare 177
Chapter 28: Why You Wanna Trip On Me. 185
Chapter 29: The Rebirth 197
Thank You 217
Phoenix Rising 221

The Legacy

The Jacksons... a legacy of music, a legacy of brotherhood that has made record breaking ***History*** in the world of entertainment. The Jackson brothers, Jackie, Tito, Jermaine, Marlon, Michael, and Randy, have come together in ***Triumph*** to bring forth the power of their unity. At a very young age, these men strived for perfection and persevered all the obstacles to meet their ***Destiny***. Now, the Jacksons' success is their ***Victory*** as they unite in fellowship for the power of the brotherhood. Their extraordinary talent remains unsurpassed as no one can ever compare to the fame and success of this legendary family. And so the Jackson legacy continues, through their children, and through their music.

The dream goes on...

Prelude

Awesome! I couldn't believe my eyes! Nothing could have prepared me for what I had just witnessed. I sat on the floor in front of our floor model TV with my mouth gaping open and my eyes fixated on the TV screen watching what was about to influence me for the rest of my life. I was mesmerized — this was the greatest thing I had ever seen in my whole life! I was watching "The Ed Sullivan Show" and these five young brothers from Gary, Indiana just blew me away with their dance steps, their costumes, their energy, their screaming fans! This was the national television debut of the Jackson Five and I'll never forget it. As the Jackson brothers performed a great rendition of Sly and the Family Stone's song entitled "Stand," their funky choreographed steps and perfectly harmonized singing had captivated me. As I watched the young, lead singer, better known as Michael Jackson, pour his heart out to the lyrics of Smokey Robinson and the Miracles' hit song "Who's Loving You," I could only imagine the hysterical girls screaming and going crazy over him! I knew right then and there that I wanted to be a "star," just like one of the Jackson Five. After experiencing and seeing what effect the Jackson Five had on their fans, I realized at age 5 that this is what I wanted to do with my life. I wanted to do what they did: make people *happy*, bringing fulfillment and joy, to my adoring, screaming fans all over the world.

From that moment on, I became a true fan, tuning in to every television show that they were appearing on, including their own Saturday morning cartoons, and buying fan magazines and everything else I could find with their names plastered on it. I remember eating bowls upon bowls of cereal just to get to the cut out cardboard record of the Jackson Five on the back of the box! And fighting with my 7 siblings because I didn't want to share them with anyone! After all they were America's first Black, young, "Bubble gum," teen idol, heart-throbs, and above that they were gifted and talented far beyond their years. These 5 young brothers were definitely here to stay for many years to come. They put so much heart and soul into their performance, individually and collectively, and generated so much power that you couldn't help but be absorbed by their talent, charm, and love like it was osmosis. I thank God for the Jacksons because their American Dream was a dream come true. I thank all of the Jacksons for making the dream a reality because I have been *touched by the Jacksons.*

CHAPTER 1
In The Beginning...

The best times of my life were with my family on Friday nights. I *loved* Friday nights. My father used to come visit us every weekend after work on Friday because he and my mother had separated when I was only five years old. But even though they were separated, they spent the weekends together and always made sure the family remained close. The whole family would be together; my brothers and sisters, all eight of us, starting with Charles, the oldest, then Rosalind, Bruce, Jacqueline, Steven, Donald, Suzette, and me, the "baby," along with my mother and father. My father, Frank, would bring home bags of food to cook for everyone all weekend, including my favorite big Sunday breakfast—eggs, bacon, grits, waffles, you name it! He enjoyed cooking for everyone and, nothing against my mother's cooking, but he could really "throw down" in the kitchen! He would bring us some of the latest 45 records to play on our hi-fi stereo and we would all dance and sing around the living room, while he would pick us up one by one and slow dance with us as he crooned his favorite Motown and other artists' songs in our ears, including his favorite Oldies, but goodies, and the newest hit songs. We would have so much fun that we would often fight at whose turn it was to have the next dance with our father. Being the large family that we are, everyone had to have their "spotlight" and do their thing, and my oldest brother Charles and sister Jackie used to pretend they were Marvin Gaye and Diana Ross and sing for all of us. My brother Steven, the biggest Smokey Robinson fan, would pretend he was Smokey, minus the Miracles, and sing his favorite love songs. Even though Charles and Jackie never pursued a professional singing career, they had great voices and probably could have been successful in the music industry if they put their efforts into it and worked hard together. Unfortunately, my siblings' talent was only heard by the rest of the Phoenix family. Then everyone would have to clear the dance floor and let me do my *thang*! When I would get into my Michael Jackson routine, doing my spins, struts, slides, and splits, my whole family would just go crazy and cheer for me, encourage me, and clap thunderously like I was performing in a concert hall and they were giving me a standing ovation! You couldn't tell me I wasn't Michael Jackson!

One of my favorite things my father used to do for me and his two other youngest ones, Donald and Suzette, is make us into a "swing." He would bend over, pick us up from under our knees, holding our legs like we were sitting on a "swing," and swing us back and forth, back and forth, until his back couldn't take it anymore! Time spent with my father was always special because he made it a point to do special things for each one of us and made the time for all of us.

Some weekends, when he had some extra money, my father would bring me shopping for Batman comic books, since I was a Batman fanatic! Batman was our favorite superhero, and still is, although we would read other superhero comics as well. Actually, my father enjoyed reading comic books as much as I did, and we would sit there for hours and read our comic books together. He even showed me how to turn the pages neatly and properly so I could maintain the "mint condition" that the book was in and preserve it. And when it was Christmas time, I wasn't hard to please—everyone knew exactly what to get me... *Batman toys*! If I couldn't get a particular toy, I would improvise and create my own Batman invention, like my Batman cape that I made from an ordinary bathroom towel. My mother would tie it around my neck and I'd be off and running, singing "**Da na na na na na na na na na na na na na na, BATMAN!**" I remember every Wednesday and Thursday evening at 7:30 P.M., I would tune in to my favorite Bat-capade on television with two straight days of "Batman," starring Adam West and Burt Ward, and Thursday's episode was always the cliffhanger. If you saw Thursday's show, you just couldn't wait to see next Wednesday's concluding episode! It was like an ongoing saga in Batman and Robin's fight against crime! And when I would sit down and watch my favorite show in the whole world, "Batman," I would hush everybody and tell them "Shut up and stop talking while I'm watching 'Batman'!"—me, the youngest, spoiled little brat in the house! And they let me get away with that, too!

I was born May 9, 1964, in Brooklyn, New York, the youngest of eight children. I was a pest, a brat, a tattletale; your average "runt" of the family. And so befitting of my character, my oldest brother Charles nicknamed me "Runt," which I am still known as to this day! Even my nieces and nephews refer to me affectionately as "Uncle Runt." My oldest sister, Rosalind, nicknamed me "Baby," obviously because I am the youngest, but also because she would often look after me and I was sort of like her own baby to her. This nickname also stuck with me to this day, but mostly Rosalind, my mother, and my elder relatives call me that. No one in my entire family really calls me by my first name, Arthur; even my father had his own name for me—"Boy." Actually, it may seem very strange, but almost everyone in my family either is called by a nickname or their middle name; only a few of us are actually addressed by our first names. We even refer to our parents as Frank and Mary or "Mare," not Daddy and Mommy. We called our grandmother "Mom" because when my mother had her first child Charles, she was only 16 years old and my grandmother helped to raise him, and insisted he call her "Mom." So in turn, we all called her "Mom," too. My brother Charles also nicknamed my sister Rosalind, "Guy," for whatever reason, we don't remember, but the name stuck with her. And then there are the ones that are called by their middle names, like my father, Frank, whose full name is Charles *Frank*, my brother Bruce, who is really Edward *Bruce*, and my sister Suzette, whose name is Andrea *Suzette*. Any questions?

I always loved growing up in the Bedford-Stuyvesant section of Brooklyn, living in those large 3-story landmark brownstones, with the beautiful architecture, detailed wood trimming, high ceilings, shiny wood floors, extra large windows, and spacious rooms. As a child, I knew that I lived differently than the people on television; my house wasn't as "nice," or my neighborhood didn't have those big parks full of blooming spring flowers and nothing but green grass and trees everywhere, but I didn't know that I lived in what is called the "ghetto." To me it was home, and still is, for when I was growing up it certainly was not dangerous like it has become over the years, due to economic and social depreciation. It was a place that you could call "home," a place where Black people could live together in a neighborhood and it felt like one very large family living together, but in separate houses. People cared about each other. People helped one another. Children played outside without fear of being the next target of a random driveby shooting. Children could go to school without guns, knives, and razors in their pocket and not have to walk through a metal detector to get inside. People could walk down the street at any given time, night or day, and be greeted by a friendly "How are you, my brother/sister" not "Gimme your money." Black people stuck together as a "people," but over time, the thought of togetherness was replaced by selfishness and this Black "family" lifestyle has been slowly diminishing.

One thing I do remember fondly is how everyone in the neighborhood used to spread the word when a Black performing artist, whether they were currently popular, legendary or debuting for the first time, was going to be on the radio or television, and we all would listen or watch in support of our Black achievers and talk about it for days on end. This is how I found out that the Jackson Five were going to be on "The Ed Sullivan Show" for the first time, along with my sister Jackie, who was a big J-5 fan. She also told me that the Jackson Five were going to be on "Ed Sullivan," and she couldn't wait to see Jackie Jackson, her favorite brother, who was so "groovy" and "outta sight," perform on television. She always read all the popular Black teen fanzines, such as <u>Right On!</u>, <u>Ebony Jr</u>, and <u>Black Star</u>, or any other publication that featured the Jackson Five, and was the first person to introduce me to the Jackson Five. I was only five at the time, so just seeing their photos in a magazine wasn't enough to convince me of their talent—I had to see them "live!" So on that historical eve of December 14, 1969, Sunday night at 8:00 P.M. on the CBS network, my entire family, including my neighborhood family, gathered around the living room to watch *history* being born—the national debut of the world's now most famous, most talented, most widely recognized and publicized Black family in entertainment *history*—the Jackson Five, or currently known as *The Jacksons*. The next day, everyone was proudly raving about the Jackson Five's performance the previous night; my friends, my neighbors, my school teachers, my family… and they didn't stop talking about them. The news had spread uptown, downtown, all around the town about these talented young men. There was definitely something uniquely special about these young brothers from Gary, Indiana. Some people were comparing them to Frankie Lymon and the Teenagers, who had a promising career that was shortened by the death of the lead singer, Frankie Lymon, whose life was tragically ended by a fatal drug overdose. But the talent of the Jackson Five superseded all of the other "kid" or family acts, then to now, throughout music *history*. They were so well-rehearsed, polished, exciting, confident; their stage presence alone was so outstanding and powerful, it was like they reached out off the stage and grabbed hold of you by your shirt, pulling you towards them as they hypnotized you with their choreographed dancing and harmonized singing. From that instant moment of fame, the Jacksons' career has taken flight and hasn't landed since. It has soared so high, it is like a satellite in orbit and may never return to this earth!

    This is where you could say my career also began. I wanted to be just like one of the Jacksons and put every moment of spare time I could find into practicing my dancing and singing. I would run home after school to my "solo" Jackson rehearsal, trying to imitate every note of every song that my sister Jackie and I owned, trying to perfect every dance step of every song I saw the Jackson Five perform on television. Back in those days, we didn't have VCRs to record our favorite shows on videotape; we had to rely on our memory and imagination. I take pride in the fact that I had a photographic memory when it came to remembering, in detail, each and every one of the Jackson Five's performances that I had seen on television. Of course, my photographic memory was only limited to Jackson Five performances—it didn't include my schoolwork or chores at home! I had a one-track mind and a goal, and that was what my mind was focused on at all times. When I was locked in my room pretending to be one of the Jacksons, I would put on an entire "concert" for my imaginary audience, but had to have my homemade microphone and stand for authenticity. I would take the wooden stick that is in the bottom part of your average window shade that you pull up and down and saw it down to my desired microphone length. (Yes, I would put back the sawed-off piece back in the shade, hoping no one would notice.) I would then ball up a sheet of tinfoil and attach it to the end of my stick creating my microphone. My microphone wire would be the cord from the venetian blinds, which I also cut off myself hoping no one would notice, and would tape it to my microphone. For the finishing touch, I would add my microphone stand—an old curtain rod that was bent and couldn't be used on a window anymore and, **WALA!**—I was "live" and "in concert!" I never used a mirror during my rehearsals; I always relied on instinct and feeling the dance moves. I knew when I didn't do something exactly right because it didn't feel right. I was very much in tune with the Jacksons and my own body and would envision myself in the body of a Jackson doing the choreographed routines, perfecting every step.

At this time in my life, my entire existence, was basically centered around the Jackson Five. Their songs were blaring out of radios and stereo hi-fis all throughout the neighborhood, especially my house, and the one song that stands out in my mind as the song that best represents them or identifies them as being the infamous Jackson Five is "The Love You Save." I heard that song nonstop for months, from sunup to sundown, everywhere I went, people young and old were playing it and listening to it. It was like the Jackson Five's own "National

Anthem!"

As I previously mentioned, my sister Jackie used to buy all of the popular Black "fanzines" that featured the Jackson Five—Ebony, Right On!, Jet, etc., and would read the articles and stories to me, since I was too young to read them myself. Even if she was out with her friends all day, when she came home for the evening, she would always try to have a new magazine for us and would sit down and read to me until it was time to go to bed. It was my nightly bedtime story!

My family knew how much I loved the Jacksons and because I was too young to know how to find out when the Jacksons where going to be on television, I had everyone in my household on "Jackson Patrol." They used to look for commercials, read the TV Guide listings, and listen to the radio for any shows that featured the Jackson Five for me. If the Jacksons were going to be on a show that was past my bedtime, no matter how late it was, my mother always let me stay up to watch, even when they were on "The Late Show" starring Johnny Carson! As I reminisce on how spoiled I was, I recall the time my mother stayed awake for two days straight watching "The Jerry Lewis Telethon" the year of 1974, waiting for the Jackson Five to appear! All that waiting was worth it to her because she saw the gleam in my eye when I finally saw the Jackson Five's performance of their number one hit, "Dancin' Machine," after waiting for two days! Only a mother would sacrifice for her child the way she did for me.

CHAPTER 2
Bridge Over Troubled Water

It took me years to learn why my parents separated in 1969. Sure they didn't see eye to eye on some things and would argue like most parents do. I'm sure it was tough supporting and raising eight kids with a blue-collar job income coming from just my father. He worked hard and liked to drink (alcohol) on the weekends, "too much" according to my mother, and that caused more stress between them, too. But one particular Sunday night they got into a heated argument, over what exactly, I wasn't aware of at the time, but I do remember my mother was more upset than usual at my father. Things simmered down before they went to bed, but the next day, while my father was at work, my mother packed up all his clothes in brown paper bags and put them outside the front door. When my father came home and noticed all his things sitting outside waiting for him, he knocked on the door first before coming in the house, anticipating my mother's anger. My mother went flying to the door, ranting and raving at him over what he had "done," telling him "you ain't allowed in this house no more!" My father, a man of few words, quietly begged and pleaded with my mother to let him back in the house because this was his home as well as her home. My mother had an awful temper and calmed down just enough to let my father in the house—but only to get the rest of his things! Again, I didn't know it at the time, but the reason my mother was so infuriated with my father that she made him leave the house was because she discovered he was having an affair. I can't speak for my father, but I personally believe my mother's ways led him astray from her. My mother always put unnecessary pressure on my father and complained over every stinking thing, just for the sake of complaining. She was never satisfied and just couldn't let sleeping dogs lie sometimes. I felt compassion for him at times because I knew how hard he worked and tried to do all that he could as a father, a provider, and a role model for his children. My mother just did not know how to keep a good thing and be *happy* for herself or her family. You know the old saying, "Misery loves company." That's the best way to describe my mother's ways.

Well, misery came to her when my oldest brother, Charles, enlisted into the United States Army in 1968. He and a few of his friends got a brainstorm idea that the "chicks" would dig them in their Army uniforms, so they went to the local Recruitment Office and enlisted! They thought it would be so easy—just six weeks of basic training and then they could leave! Well, it doesn't work that way in the Army, as most of us know. My mother was dead set against Charles going into the Army, but it was too late—there was nothing she could do. This was during the time of the Vietnam War and she felt that the Government was sending our young, inexperienced men off to war without the proper training and preparation, both mentally and physically. These young men didn't even know why they were fighting this war for another country. I don't like to get too political about the Vietnam War, but my general opinion about war itself is that we all should follow the famous words of the late John Lennon and "Give Peace A Chance" because "All You Need Is Love."

Charles finally returned home after the grueling 6-8 weeks of Basic Training and had no intentions of going back after his leave. My mother was so distraught over the thought of her first son going off to war, she somehow managed to convince the Army "Officials" that she needed Charles at home with her since he was her oldest son and could help her maintain the family household. She told them she needed him to work and provide an income for the family since my father had moved out of the house and her Welfare checks weren't enough to support her seven other children. My father was still living at home with us during this time, but my mother was desperate and would have said or done anything to keep her son at home. With God's blessing, the Army dismissed Charles and he was able to stay home with us permanently. But he brought home with him a "momento"; something that was never in our house before, something that was a sign of the times, and that "something" was *heroin*. This thing, this fiend, this beast, caused a great deal of problems for my family. My four oldest siblings, Charles, Rosalind, Bruce, and Jackie, were all teen-agers at the time and like most average teen-agers, were influenced by peer pressure and trying to be cool, and decided to experiment with this new drug. And without my father in the house to keep everyone in line, it made the experimentation all the more enticing. Unfortunately, the experimenting turned to addiction for three of them, Charles included, and he ended up in and out of jail a few times for minor offenses because of it.

    Heroin came to the Phoenix family and wreaked havoc, leading a path of destruction, until the day of the "final conflict." This was one of the scariest moments in my life and I will never, ever forget it. One weekday morning in 1970, my mother sent my brother Donald to get everyone to come into the kitchen to eat breakfast that she had prepared. When he went to get Charles, who was sound asleep, he could not wake him up. He started shoving and pushing him in the bed, and even screamed in his ear to wake him up, but nothing happened. My brother had had a heroin overdose and was unconscious. Donald, in a panic-stricken frenzy, began to scream uncontrollably and my mother dropped the dish in her hand and ran into Charles' room like a bolt of lightning. I don't know how she did it, but somehow she managed to wake Charles up and revive him out of unconsciousness. At the precise moment, the whole house became silent and just stared into midair because we were all so scared and shocked at what had just happened. Once my mother was sure Charles was sober, she began crying, yelling, and hitting Charles out of anger for putting her, and the entire family, through this horrifying ordeal. After the storm had passed, she embraced him lovingly, and thanked the Lord for saving her son. I was so shaken up by this incident, almost seeing my brother die in front of my eyes, that I vowed to never, ever, take any kind of "drug," or smoke cigarettes or marijuana, in my lifetime. I'm very proud to say that I've lived up to the promise to myself and God and never have gone back on that promise. I believe in nourishing the body, the mind, and the soul, not poisoning it.

    My oldest sister, Rosalind, or better known as "Guy" (remember the nickname thing), rocked the boat so badly with the news of her pregnancy, that I thought my house was the Titanic and it was sinking fast! I was *happy* at least—I became a proud uncle for the first time in 1967, at the age of three, and many times thereafter. Guy had her first child, a girl named Joette, at the age of 18, but the time during her pregnancy caused turmoil in the household. Once the news hit my father, he blew his top, which for my father was a rarity, and started fighting with my mother about how could this have happened.

"Why was Guy doing drugs?" (more fuel on the fire), "Weren't you watching over her?," "Why didn't you tell her?"... It went on and on for months. Each parent blamed the other for all of this and were too eager to point the finger at one another, without stopping to evaluate the situation more closely. They were starting to go through some changes around this time themselves and, unfortunately, overlooked the warning signals of what was happening until it just happened! The bickering finally settled down between my parents and they tried to work things out and keep the family together, especially because of all their children and their first grandchild on the way! Honestly, it's not a healthy thing to stay together for the childrens' sake because everyone is miserable and neither parent wants to take the blame for the family falling apart at the seams. But my parents did manage to stay together for two more years, probably because they were so proud to become grandparents for the first time and share that joy together!

The happiest times for all of us were during the holidays, particularly Christmas time; the spirit of the season was so enrapturing that you couldn't help but be hypnotized by it! Everyone was so generous, kind, and loving towards one another, it made the holiday time even more special. My parents didn't have a lot of money to go around to buy presents for all 8 of their children, but they made sure they gave you at least one thing that you hoped and prayed and asked Santa Claus for! On Christmas morning, when we came into the living room where the tree was, our parents had put our presents under the tree, in individual piles, unwrapped (why waste all that time and paper?), so we knew exactly which pile was ours! But when I say "pile," I don't mean a huge pile, I mean just a few choice presents that we desired! Well for me, you know what that was—*Batman toys*! It was great fun to have opened boxes spread out all over the house on Christmas day—made it look like Santa dropped a few sacks full of presents in our house! These were really the best times of my life, and my siblings as well, because we were all together as a family, especially my parents, and we were *happy* to have each other.

I also loved Halloween for the obvious reasons—Halloween candy and my big chance to *really* be Batman in a real Batman costume! Remember those plastic 1-piece costumes with the coordinating plastic masks that had the elastic that goes around the back of the head, with holes cut out for the eyes, nose, and mouth? They were the best! I put that costume on first thing in the morning and wore it all day until it was time for bed. The only thing I didn't like about Halloween was that my mother didn't allow me to go trick-or-treating; I could only go to my neighbors house that we knew very well and that's it. At the time, there was a lot of talk to take every precaution on Halloween because some crazy people were trying to put poison in the candy or stick razor blades in the apples, and I think my mother really was a little too overprotective about it. Either that or she just didn't want to bring us trick-or-treating. But now that I'm a father, I live Halloween through my children and look forward to taking them trick-or-treating every year to get loads of candy in their favorite costumes!

When money got a little tight for my mother in taking care of all her children, she would sometimes play Bingo or cards to try to win more money, double or triple what she had. She was very lucky at cards and sometimes at Bingo. I remember her staying up all weekend playing cards with her "card parties" when times got really hard for her. Sometimes it got a little rough surviving on just my father's salary and my mother's Welfare, but she did what she had to do. And boy, she was good. She was a real card shark; if my mother was in a movie playing cards with Kenny Rogers, she would have been "The Gambler" and whipped the pants off of him! As we were growing up, we all watched and learned from her and would challenge each other in a game of cards. We used to like to play Gin Rummy, Knuckles, Pitty-Pat, and War. We also liked to play other games such as Monopoly, the Batman board game, Hide-and-Seek, and on those bad weather days, baseball in the house! Of course we all loved to play baseball, football, whatever the game, outside, but on those frosty winter days when it was just too cold or snowy outside, or on those gloomy, rainy days when the sun was nowhere to be found, we had no choice but to play inside the house together. But baseball got us into too much trouble, so we had to keep that game outside, because once you start running around trying to hit and catch the aluminum foil "baseball," you're so busy trying to beat the other team that you end up knocking things over. Mom always said, "Don't play ball in the house!" That's when the game ended—once something got broken, no matter who did it, we all got an ass-whipping for it because we shouldn't have been playing rough in the house. I'm not talking about a slap on the butt, I'm talking about an "ass-whipping," with a whipping device! As most Black people can tell you, **"The Belt"** was the most feared item in the household, along with the extension cord and the Hot Wheel Tracks, which can burn some mean rubber on your behind! First, you would get disciplined with the shouting and hollering, and if that wasn't enough to do the job, then out came "The Belt." In all the times that my father disciplined me, I remember only getting "The Belt" three times, because when it comes to my father, you don't play around. His whippings lasted for days on your butt;

in other words, "a hard head makes a sore ass."

And if you thought my mother and father were strict, which they were, then you haven't met "Mom," my grandmother! She was set in her ways and acted like a drill sergeant with us, always keeping us in line under her regime. My mother went into the hospital in 1969 for a miscarriage, and "Mom" came to stay with us to take care of the household, along with my father. In actuality, my mother had a total of 15 pregnancies, but only eight children survived. All three of her girls survived with a healthy delivery, and the others that didn't survive were all boys, including the last miscarriage she had in 1969. I guess she somehow knew deep inside her, like a mother's instinct, that I was going to be her last child, her "Baby," because she always called me that since I was an infant. Even though my sister, Guy, gave me the nickname, my mother never called any of her other children "Baby"—they all had their own nicknames.

My grandmother, the "Sergeant," would walk in the door handing out the orders and rules for us. We had to limit all our utilities and necessities; only one light on in the entire house after dark, don't keep the TV on all day, and use the water sparingly. I was only allowed to watch the "Batman" TV series and my Saturday morning cartoons—nothing else! Since my mother babied me too much, and of course I played into it, I was unable to shake my habit of drinking a bottle until I was five years old! Oh yes! I used to come in from playing outside, all parched from running around, and couldn't wait to hit that bottle filled with ice cold milk or juice! And when my grandmother walked in the door to lay down the law, she came towards me saying "First things first" and took my bottle and hid it from me! Oh no, *how could she do this?* I needed that bottle! I couldn't live without that bottle! I had to call my mother in the hospital, with the help of my sister, and tell her to talk Mom into giving me my bottle back. What a brat, huh. Thank God, it worked—I got my bottle back and life was sweet! Eventually, another year later, I finally kicked the habit and gave the bottle the boot!

TOUCHED BY THE JACKSONS

CHAPTER 3
We're Here To Entertain You

My family had moved to Covert Street in the Bushwick section of Brooklyn in 1971 and that's where I met my first little "girlfriend" and was smitten by puppy love. Her name was Denise and she lived up the block from me. I befriended her brother, Stevie, and whenever we would play together, she would always try to jump into whatever we were playing—Tag, Hide-and-Seek, or board games. Denise was a big Jackson Five fan, just like her three older sisters who loved Jermaine, Jackie, and Marlon Jackson, and knew how much I liked the Jacksons, too. I knew that she really like me because she kept coming around me constantly while I was playing with her brother, Stevie, but I just ignored her. Then one day when we were all playing Tag outside with a bunch of kids on the street, she gave me my first kiss! I was "It" at the time, and when I caught her and tagged her, she turned to me in the heat of the moment and planted one right on my lips! How embarrassing! She was always very sassy and definitely not shy, and after she gave me my first kiss, asked me to be her boyfriend. And like a fool, blinded by love, with my nose wide open like a two-car garage, I said "yes!"

My desire to impress females started with Denise, and I wanted to show off and buy gifts for her to prove what a wonderful boyfriend I was! And like a fool again, every Friday I got a thirty-cent allowance and this week I wanted to impress my "Sweet Thing" with the dough. On that faithful Saturday morning, I got up early, even skipped all my favorite Saturday morning cartoons, including "The Jackson Five" cartoon, and ran up the block to her house to display my wealth of 3 dimes to my sweetheart! I felt so rich, like I was J.D. Rockefeller, and without any hesitation, she quickly snatched the money from my hand! She ran out the front door, with me right behind her, up to the candy store on the corner to spend our loot on all the candy she wanted. Other kids from the block were in there buying candy too, so when we got back in front of her house, everyone started playing and eating their candy, except me. I was the only one without any and when I asked my true love to share with me, she flat out said "NO!" I nicely reminded her that I bought her the candy with my money and she said "Don't be an Indian giver!" She wouldn't give me a piece of anything! And when I went to help myself to a piece, she took it from my hand and spit in my face! In front of everyone! She made me feel like the size of an ant and I just walked away and went over to play with the boys.

    The following week, Miss Stingy came to my house on Saturday morning to ask me to come outside and play with her. Smitten by love and foolishness, I followed behind my Sweet Thing, with thirty-cents in my pocket, and took Denise to the candy store once again. This time we shared all the candy because I didn't let it out of my hands for a second! After a while, it became a weekly habit and my sister Jackie told me to stop buying her candy because all Denise was doing was using me for my money. I finally saw the light of day when my money ran out, the candy ran out, and Denise ran out! Seems like her mother taught her too young and too well how to use a man for his money. To this very day, she's probably draining some other poor fool right now! I got off easy with thirty-cents a week!

Now that I had my first girlfriend, I wanted to always look sharp and be cool like my older brothers. My brother Steven, whom I considered my coolest brother, taught me how to keep my clothes pressed and creased, comb and pick out my J-5 afro, maintain proper "manly" hygiene, and not to cry when he would comb out "the kitchen," the naps in the back of my head. For a while, he was my closest and, dare I say, favorite brother at this time, even though we would still fight like cats and dogs. He had a great knack for teasing me and knew just how to piss me off, so he would do it as often as possible! He and my oldest brother, Charles, used to be pimpin' with the latest threads; big brimmed hats, platform shoes, corduroy coats with fur-trimmed collars, big-ass bell bottoms, polyester shirts—they were looking "sharp as a mosquito!" They were dressing even cooler than the guys on "Soul Train!" This was the first year "Soul Train" debuted on television and it was the first Black television show featuring Black performing artists and Black amateur dancers doing all the latest steps to the latest Soul/R & B hits. It was sometimes the only show that would provide exposure and display up and coming Black artists for its Black viewing audience across the United States. "Soul Train" has become an icon in television *history*, as well as music *history*, as the longest running Black entertainment program—over a quarter of a century and still going strong! *You can bet your last money, honey!*

Another close friend of mine, Clifford, lived up the street from me and was a big Jermaine Jackson fan. He thought Jermaine was the coolest because he was the first Black teen idol/sex symbol and got all the chicks! We used to sit in his room and listen to his *Maybe Tomorrow* album and pretend that we were the Jackson Five. I was Michael, with my hairbrush microphone, and he was Jermaine, with his broomstick bass guitar! We had a lot of fun together! I'll never forget the night of April 18, 1971, "The Diana Ross Special" was on TV and I watched it over at Clifford's house, not only because he was my friend, but because the landlord of our house didn't pay the electric bill and our electricity was cut off temporarily (we also didn't have heat, but both problems were resolved in about a week). The Jackson Five were her special guests on the show and the next day, all the kids at school and in the neighborhood were talking about how "outta sight" they were! Clifford and I couldn't stop talking about them either! We had new routines to learn! Years ago, Black entertainers—actors, dancers, singers, musicians, etc., were not on many television shows, so when someone was going to be on a show, or a "special" particularly, it was even more rare and made it more exciting to see. Just like when the Jackson Five had their first television special, "Goin' Back To Indiana," that was one of the best performances the Jackson Five ever gave and it was right in their home town of Gary, Indiana. They put on such a dynamite show that I have never seen another young family or "kid" act even come close to the Jackson Five's level of performance... *When they were tiny little boys, they used to dance, they used to sing, before they even learned to crawl or walk...* The Sylvers, The Osmonds brothers, whoever, could not stack up to the Jackson Five by any means. The Jacksons were pros; they had been worked by their father Joseph Jackson to the point of perfection. As they were struggling to make it big, they played anywhere and everywhere, from schools, to nightclubs, to topless bars... you name it! The Jackson brothers have seen it all with their young eyes! Whatever it took to get his boys out there, that's what Joe Jackson did for his sons. And it paid off. There were times when they were performing at certain nightclubs, people would just throw money up on the stage for them because they were so talented, what else could they do! Marlon said that when people threw money at them, it was usually dollar bills and some coins, which would often add up to more than they got paid for the booking itself! He and Michael used to pick up most of the money, doing splits and picking up money from the floor at the same time. They were pretty slick! I can probably bet that the Sylvers or the Osmonds never experienced anything like that.

It's very interesting how the music industry works and creates a group or an artist as a commodity to market to the public for a quick profit. This is how the Osmonds were marketed; they were the "White" version of the Jackson Five that the music industry created to market to their White audience. The enormous success of the Jackson Five, a Black family group, put a foot in the door for the Osmonds, who were a White family group reflective of the Jackson Five, with their 5 family members, all brothers, and a lead singer who was the youngest and the "cutest" of them all. The only problem was the Osmond brothers were not that talented, couldn't dance at all, and just did not have that gifted star quality that the Jacksons were blessed with. Their vocal talents lacked the harmony, rhythm and soulfulness that the Jackson brothers possessed. The Jackson Five proved themselves as the world's most famous Black performing group in *history* and have had so much success individually and collectively since then that no other group compares! As far as it goes with those other groups from yesteryear, those fly-by-night groups, where are they today? You might find them working in dead end joints, trying to make their way in the entertainment industry. The Jacksons are special—they are the "chosen" ones. They have pulled the sword from the stone in *victory*.

"Long, long ago, the Black children had no one to look

up to. They were lost without any good music to listen to. It was said that whatever young, Black group would pull the sword from the stone, would be kings, for years and years. It was prophesied that the Jacksons would come and pull the sword from the stone and would prevail and stand the test of time. The Jacksons would be called Great, Most Holy, and Powerful. Their kingdom shall be a kingdom that will never be brought to ruin. It will last for time indefinite 'til time indefinite because the Jacksons pulled the sword from the stone."

> *"The Jacksons claimed their way*
> *And they're here to stay*
> *The Jacksons are the best, better than all the rest.*
> *Working night to day*
> *No time to play*
> *Just family*
> *Jackie, Tito, Marlon, Michael, Jermaine, Randy*
> *The dream goes on...*
> *Arise all the world and behold the Jacksons!"*

CHAPTER 4
Jackson-mania!!

The Jacksons' eminent reign flourished across the nation and caused such hysteria that the only way to describe it is "Jackson-Mania." Everywhere you looked, everywhere you turned, all you saw and heard was the Jackson Five—they were on posters, T-shirts, magazines, buttons, albums, cereal boxes, lunch boxes, radios, record players, television shows, television commercials—everything was stamped with the royal "J-5" crest! Remember those famous Post cereal commercial endorsements for Honeycomb and Alpha Bits, with J-5 singing the Alpha Bits jingle to the tune of their hit, "ABC?" And the J-5 cardboard records on the back of the cereal box that you had to cut out yourself and fight with your brothers and sisters over who had "dibs" on it first! They were a great novelty, but the sound quality was certainly not of vinyl standards.

The Jackson craze, hysteria, "invasion," was comparable to the British Invasion of the Fab Four and the "Beatlemania" that swept across the country less than a decade before. The obvious difference is that the Jacksons are brothers, they're American, and they're Black. The Jackson Five sat on their throne the year of 1972 and ruled the entire nation with their amazing talent and overwhelming success. They dominated the charts with their multiple album releases; the Jackson Five's *Lookin' Through The Window* and their *Greatest Hits*, which was released December 1971, Jermaine's first solo album, *Jermaine*, Michael's first solo album, *Got To Be There*, in 1971, and his second release, *Ben*, in 1972, which was the theme song for the motion picture of the same name. The Jacksons also flooded the charts and the airwaves with their numerous single releases that year—J5's "Sugar Daddy," released in December 1971, the title cut "Lookin' Through The Window," 1972, and "Corner Of The Sky" from the Broadway musical *Pippin'* in 1973, Jermaine's "That's How Love Goes" and "Daddy's Home," both released in 1972, Michael's title cut "Got To Be There," "Rockin' Robin," "I Wanna Be Where You Are," and "Ben," which was a Golden Globe Award winner and an Academy Award nomination. "I Wanna Be Where You Are" became a hit single and the flip side "We've Got A Good Thing Going," which never topped the charts, went on to become the "unofficial" theme song for teen-agers that were in love. "I Wanna Be Where You Are" was also one of my father's all-time favorite songs by the Jackson Five and every time I hear it, I think of him fondly.

Jermaine's popularity among the female fans was growing bigger and bigger as his loyal fans made it very well known who their favorite Jackson brother was by screaming his name at every given public opportunity. Even all the fan magazines were promoting Jermaine's individual celebrity status! They touted Michael as being young and cute, but Jermaine was "sexy." Jermaine's good looks and soulful voice warranted him the prestigious title of America's 1st Black Teen Idol, especially after the release of "I Found That Girl," which was the flip side to the 1970 hit, "The Love You Save." I always remember the infamous "Jackson Five" cartoon episode with cartoon-Jermaine singing with his cartoon brothers, "Momma, I think I found that girl..." But his hit "Daddy's Home" proved him as a successful solo artist. And this was only the beginning! The Jackson Five made numerous appearances on popular television shows, such as "The Flip Wilson Show," "The Carol Burnett Show," "Soul Train," "American Bandstand," "The Sonny and Cher Show," "Hellzapoppin'," the British show, "Top Of The Pops," their own second TV special, "The Jackson Five Show," and the film documentary, *Save The Children*. Even little Michael Jackson made a special appearance on the famous "Dating Game" show. He was the special celebrity guest in search of a date, interviewing his panel of young ladies trying their best to win a date with Michael Jackson! And his *little bitty pretty one* was a sweet young girl named Venus, as in the Goddess of Love! The Jackson brothers were also going to star in their first feature film, produced by Raymond St. Jacques, starring Bill Cosby and Cicely Tyson, but the project never materialized. The Jackson Five also played a Royal Command performance for the Queen of England and embarked on their first European Tour. And just when you thought it was impossible for the Jackson brothers to have any free time left for themselves, let alone share time with someone besides one of their brothers, Tito found the time to get married! He was the first Jackson brother to marry, taking Miss Delores ("Dee Dee") Martes to be his lawfully wedded wife in 1972, during the midst of this Jackson-Mania madness!

    All this Jackson-Mania had me in Jackson-Heaven, and I couldn't get enough of it! I, like every other Jackson maniac, male or female, had to have everything I saw with the Jackson Five on it from my lunch box, to my cereal boxes, to my T-shirts, to my buttons and posters, etc. I even had to dress like I was one of the Jackson Five—I had my big afro, the "Applejack" hat that Michael wore on the cover of his *Got To Be There* album, the big multicolored bell bottom pants with matching shirts/vests, and groovy leather shoe-boots. You couldn't tell me I wasn't a Jackson brother! I was working hard every day rehearsing and learning all the new songs and dance routines just in case one of the Jacksons got sick and they needed a replacement brother, I would be **READY**! A dream you say.... perhaps, but that dream was what kept me going and gave me the will and desire to perfect my talents. Sure there were a lot of Jackson "wanna-bes" out there trying to look like one of the Jacksons or sing and dance like one of them; hell, who didn't want to be just like the Jackson Five? Guys wanted to look and dress like them so they would be considered cool and get all the chicks! Up and coming groups in the music industry wanted to sing like them, dance like them, act like them, hoping for the same, if not larger, success than the Jackson Five had. Their wholesome, clean-cut, "family" image also was a major factor in their mass public appeal. Everyone was trying to imitate them in one way or another, but of course, no one could be exactly like the Jackson Five. But they tried!

    The "Bubble gum" Pop music that was born from the Jackson Five started a music trend that was imitated by practically everyone during the early Seventies and was loved by people of all ages. It was fun, bouncy, clean, finger-snapping, toe-tapping, enjoyable music that everyone loved to hear. We all remember the Osmond Brothers, who were marketed to the public by their record company as the "White" version of the Jackson Five. But let's not forget the Sylvers, who were a very large Black family, like the Jacksons, that were about the closest to the Jacksons that any group act came as far as emulating the Jackson Five and being successful. The Sylvers could dance and sing, and had the biggest afros in the business by far! They were a talented group overall, but the one thing they lacked was that special one-in-a-million "star" quality that the Jacksons possessed. The Sylvers had a string of hits over the years like "Boogie Fever," "Cotton Candy" and "Hot Line," but it just wasn't enough to compete with the Jackson Five's gold and platinum fame. Even youngest brother Foster Sylvers had a successful hit, "Misdemeanor," which many people mistook him for Michael Jackson because his voice bore an uncanny likeness to Michael's vocals, and he later joined the act with his famous brothers and sisters.

Here's a trivia question for you—which Sylvers brother was one of the character voices for "The Jackson Five" cartoon series? Answer—the Sylvers' lead singer, Edmund Sylvers, was one of the famed Jackson brothers' voices for their "Jackson Five" cartoon series. The Jacksons were too busy with their careers at the time to do the voices themselves so Edmund got the opportunity to "portray" one of the Jacksons in animation! Another Sylvers brother, Leon Sylvers III, achieved his own notoriety and success by arranging and producing for an array of R & B artists such as The Whispers, Lakeside, Shalimar, and the group Dynasty, which Leon was also a member.

The Jackson-Mania carried over into 1973 as the Jackson brothers continued their endless work at maintaining their "superstar" status. The Jackson Five embarked on their first tour of Japan and then went on to Australia and New Zealand. Their worldwide popularity and fame was growing at such a phenomenal rate that they couldn't keep up with the demands themselves. Again they dominated the music charts with their multiple album and single releases, individually and as a group. Jackie Jackson released his first solo album entitled *Jackie*, which featured the hit song "Love Don't Want To Leave." Jermaine released his second solo album, *Come Into My Life*, which proved to be another success for him as a solo performer. Michael was already up to album number three, *Music & Me*, which was based on Broadway Motion Picture soundtrack hits such as "Morning Glow," the theme song of the Broadway play

Pippin', "Happy" from the motion picture, *Lady Sings The Blues*, and "With A Child's Heart," a very mature-sounding, inspiring song that is one of my all-time favorite songs by Michael. Let's not forget the Jackson Five who had two album releases this year as well, *Skywriter* and *Get It Together*. "Hallelujah Day" from the *Skywriter* album, which was originally the flip side to the single "You Made Me What I Am," became a big hit for the Jacksons. The single, "Corner Of The Sky" from the *Skywriter* album was used as the theme song for the United States Air Force in their television recruitment commercials. *Get It Together* was a step out of the "Bubble gum" sound and into a more adult, dance-style sound. The Jackson Five were maturing themselves and wanted their music to reflect their coming of age. After all, Jackie, Tito, and Jermaine were all adults over the age of 18 and Marlon and Michael weren't too far behind! The Jackson Five had to outgrow that childlike, "Bubble gum" sound in order to gain a larger audience of fans, specifically adults, and maintain the success level they've achieved. How could the Jackson Five survive in the industry if they continued to focus on the "teenybopper" fans and music, and not take their music to another level that appealed to a broader, more adult audience? Simple—they never would have survived because you have to follow the ever-changing flow of the course of music and their younger fans would have outgrown them eventually, along with their "kiddy" sound.

With their coming of age came a second marriage in the Jackson family; Jermaine Jackson married Hazel Gordy, daughter of Motown Records' founder and President, Berry Gordy. The gala affair at the Beverly Hills hotel, which overflowed with champagne, caviar, and over 500 guests, including celebrities such as Diana Ross, Marvin Gaye, Lola Falana, and Smokey Robinson, was reportedly one of the

JACKSON-MANIA!!

"poshest" in entertainment *history*. Family friend, Smokey Robinson, even composed and sang a song entitled "Wedding Song" exclusively for Jermaine and Hazel. Berry Gordy spared no costs for the celebrated event which reportedly ran him over $300,000, a lot of money for 1973 standards, even for the Motown mogul himself. In order to clarify the expenditures, the $300,000 nuptials can be compared to a million-dollar formal affair of today's highest standards. Certainly not a drop in the bucket by any means!

All my daily Jackson Five practice after school each day was beginning to pay off. My vocal style and dance techniques were being perfected as my rehearsals became more intense and focused. I was serious about performing as my whole existence was centered around it. Whether I was home, at school, or outside playing, I was eating, sleeping, and sh***ing the Jackson Five. In school, I was always getting in trouble for tapping pencils on my desk like a drum and singing J5 songs under my breath all day. My teachers would write on my report cards that "Arthur doesn't pay attention in class," "Arthur is too preoccupied with singing Jackson Five songs," and "Arthur needs to concentrate more on his schoolwork." I'll never forget, I was in a Reading Group in school in the second grade, which was designed for students that needed or wanted extra help with their reading skills, and the teacher, Miss McNeil, gave us a variety of books and magazines to choose from. Every time I went to her class, the first thing I would reach for was <u>Ebony Jr</u> magazine, instead of a regular book. I wanted to read all the news and information on Black celebrities, especially the Jackson Five. After our readings, we had to give a summary report on what we had read and I always wrote about how great the Jackson Five were, how I loved their music, and how "cool" they were. Miss McNeil took such notice to me and how

I felt about the Jackson Five and Ebony Jr magazine that she wanted me to tell the principal, Mr. Violet, how much I liked the magazine and how it gave such interesting stories on the Jackson Five and other famous Black celebrities. Mr. Violet was so impressed with my "speech" he decided to get subscriptions to Ebony Jr and other Black publications, not just for Miss McNeil's class, but for the entire student body!

One thing I remember fondly about Miss McNeil is she always used to tell us about her *younger* days when she would go to the world famous Apollo Theater in Harlem to see her favorite Black artists, particularly *Mr. Excitement* himself, the great Jackie Wilson. He was her favorite and one of mine as well. Back in the late 50's and 60's, Jackie Wilson was "The Man!" Of all the individual male performers at that time, nobody could compete or compare to the talents of Jackie Wilson. He was smooth, charming, and handsome, and had an extraordinary voice that made women faint! All the women thought he was *sooo fiiiiinne*, they would just go crazy over him! One night, the women got so out of control when Jackie was on-stage, they tore him apart trying to get a piece of his hair, his clothing... whatever they could get their hands on, and literally tore every stitch of clothing off his body, underwear and all, until he was **BUTT NAKED!!!** Can you imagine!?! Now that's **SCARY!!** It's great to have women love and adore you so much that they scream and cry for you, but to have them get so close to you that they attack you and literally tear the clothes off you, that's just scary! He's lucky all they wanted was his clothing! But Miss McNeil did enjoy telling us stories about her heydays of going to see many legendary artists perform at the Apollo almost as much as we enjoyed listening. Today when I listen to my favorite songs by Jackie Wilson such as "To Be Loved," "That's Why (I Love You So),"

"Baby Workout," "Doggin' Around," and "Your Love Keeps Lifting Me (Higher And Higher)," it raises my spirits and brings joy and happiness to my soul. But it also saddens me because of the untimeliness of his death, particularly when I hear "Lonely Teardrops." This song not only hurts me deeply, it brings tears to my eyes to know that this great performer left this universe before his time.

    Miss McNeil was an excellent teacher who tried to explain to me that I needed to be educated in everything—Reading, Math, Science, *History*, my "*ABC's*," and to broaden my horizons beyond the Jackson Five. I even got into a debate with her about it and told her I didn't need the education because I was going to grow up and be famous just like the Jackson Five. I was going to sell millions of records and make lots of money and she said "When you become famous, who's going to handle your contracts if you don't learn how to read?" I said "My manager would take care of that for me—I don't have to learn how to read." Then she said "What about your money; who's going to count your money for you?" I told her "That's what my accountant will do for me—I won't have to do it." I was a little smart-ass and thought I had the answer to everything. Miss McNeil stressed that I would have to learn how to read and write anyway to watch over my manager and accountant so I wouldn't get cheated by them. As I got older I realized that this was very wise advice and took heed to her words. Over the years, I've encountered many people in this business who tried to "sheister" me and get over on me, but of course, I didn't allow it to happen. I've seen other people in this business that have gotten sheisted, robbed, cheated, you name it, because they didn't know any better. To this day, I hold the utmost respect for this woman for giving me such sound advice and instilling the knowledge in my brain how important an education is. This is something I enforce with my own children, especially my two oldest teenage boys, and make sure they understand the importance of an education and not make the same mistakes that I have made in my life.

CHAPTER 5
Dancin' Machine

I've never seen the Jackson Five get as much television exposure in one year than they did in 1974 with the release of the single "Dancin' Machine" from the *Get It Together* album. They appeared on every major talk show, variety show, and music show there was promoting their hit. Of course, I loved every minute of it and put my Jackson-only photographic memory into overdrive with all the "Dancin' Machine" performances. The Jackson Five made appearances on practically everything from "The Mike Douglas Show," to "The Dinah Shore Show," "Soul Train," "American Bandstand," "The Sonny and Cher Show," a few television specials; they even came back and did a few shows twice in one year with their blockbuster hit and bad-ass dance routine. Truthfully, the Jacksons performed "Dancin' Machine" on every major television appearance they made from 1973 to 1976. The Jackson Five started a new trend in dancing and everyone was trying to imitate them, especially the famous "Robot" step. No, the Jacksons didn't invent the Robot; they revolutionized it. It became their signature trademark for the song "Dancin' Machine" and they had to do the Robot every time they performed that song. People expected it. And everyone would go wild when they saw the Jackson Five doing that Robot step, especially when Michael would come out in front and do his solo Robot routine. I would sit there and just study them every time I saw the Jacksons on television, implanting every move and detail in my brain on a Jackson microchip!

All my studying and rehearsals were about to pay off for me. My elementary school, P.S. 3 in Brooklyn to be exact, was having a talent show and "guess who" was gearing to hit the stage! We had several rehearsals before the actual show, but at the very first rehearsal, when I got on stage to do my thing, the song I chose was "Ben," and I put every ounce of blood and sweat into my performance. After that very first rehearsal, all the female teachers and parents that were there fell in love with me, their little "superstar," and all the little girls my age were screaming my name and were all over me like bees on honey. I'll never forget—after that first rehearsal, I got chased home by all the girls, I mean really chased all the way home! It got so bad I had to recruit some of my buddies to become my bodyguards and keep the hounds off me! Being such a big superstar, I was asked by one of my "fans" to be her boyfriend and I, of course, said yes! Her name was Monica and by coincidence, she was the talent show coordinator's daughter. But Monica wasn't enough for me—I was a celebrity now and started two-timing her, three-timing her, five-timing her... I even lost track of time I was so busy! It really started getting dangerous with the girls chasing me home from school every day because they started ripping my clothes and grabbing my hair, messin' up my cool 'fro! But two weeks before the talent show I decided to change my set from "Ben" to "Dancin' Machine." I transformed my bodyguards into my brothers (like Captain Eo) and called our group the "Action Fives!" So original!

It was finally "show time" and the Action Fives were ready to tear up that stage! The auditorium was packed with parents, their children, all the teachers, and everyone else from the neighborhood; it was a standing room only crowd! When the Action Fives first hit that stage with that "I can name that tune in…" five-beat intro of "Dancin' Machine," everyone in the audience jumped up and started clapping, dancing, and screaming for us like we were really the Jackson Five! It was incredible! The young girls in the audience were screaming so loud it was ear piercing, just like that infamous Beatles' concert at Shea Stadium where the fans were screaming so loud they drowned out the sound of the music! All you could hear were drum beats and girls screaming! You couldn't even tell what song the Beatles were singing at times because you just couldn't hear their voices over the sound of the shrieking female fans! And boy, when I did the Robot, I felt like I was in Madison Square Garden performing for 30,000 hysterical fans! The audience went wild and I felt like I was Michael Jackson himself! Never in my wildest dreams did I expect such a tremendous response from the audience like the Action Fives received. Needless to say, we were the stars of the talent show—the "superstars." It was actually a "showcase" because there weren't any winners, but it was clear to see who tore the roof off of that sucker! My life at P.S. 3 was never the same again. I had all my little groupie fans follow me around school all day and then chase me all the way home. This chasing thing went on for a long time and quite frankly, was starting to get on my nerves. I couldn't go anywhere around my neighborhood without being hounded by some teenybopper fans! I can honestly say I can relate to the stardom and fame of the Jackson Five and how they got mobbed by fans wherever they went and couldn't go out in public without a bodyguard to protect them. Being mobbed by a swarm of screaming female fans may seem exciting at first, but it can also be very scary. Sometimes they will hurt you unintentionally because of all the excitement and commotion, they don't realize their own strength when they try to hug you or get next to you while at the same time, they are trying to push the other fans away. Some people will purposely hurt you because they want some of the hair from your head, a piece of your clothing, and because you're a celebrity, all they want to do is take, take, take from you. Of course, there are the sweetest and gentlest ones out there too, but it's hard trying to decipher who's who in the crowd when there's so many people around you. Ah, the price of fame!

The following day after the talent show, our school principal even made a special announcement over the PA system, congratulating me and the Action Fives on our outstanding performance and gave special attention to my individual talent, stating that he felt like they had a "real celebrity" in their school. It was the first time the school had ever experienced such a thing with one of their young students. Thereafter, whenever one of the classes had a party in school, the teachers would invite me to perform my "Dancin' Machine" routine for everyone. I loved the opportunity to show off my talents to any audience, no matter how big or small, as long as they enjoyed the show. The screams and applause were like music to my ears, nutrients in my body, oxygen in my breath; I needed it to survive. And the more I got, the more I wanted.

I guess practically everyone in America felt the same way about the Jackson Five—the more they heard, the more they saw, the more they got from the Jackson Five, the more they wanted. Motown keenly acted on the overwhelming success of "Dancin' Machine" the single, and released an album, appropriately titled, *Dancin' Machine,* featuring the hit song, "Dancin' Machine." Other hit singles from the same album were "Whatever You Got I Want," "I Am Love" and "The Life Of The Party." The flip side to the single "Dancin' Machine," from the *Get It Together* album—"It's Too Late To

Change The Time," also became a successful hit for the Jackson Five, as they performed it on some of their television appearances. The *Save The Children* album, released by Motown, featuring an array of artists, included the Jackson Five's live performance of their hit, "I Wanna Be Where You Are." And one more Jackson brother somehow found the time to get married... Jackie Jackson, who married Enid Spann, became Jackson groom number three!

Keeping with the high demand from their fans around the world, the Jackson Five toured Africa for the first time, along with South America and the United States. And on their tour, the Jackson Five had a hot new opening act—the four member girl group, MDLT, who were managed by Mr. Joe Jackson himself. MDLT was a group of hip-swaying, longhaired, LaToya look-alikes that had two songs that were released on Ivory Tower International Records, "What's Your Game," which was written and produced by Jackie, Jermaine, Tito, Marlon, and Michael, and "Running and Pushin'," both of which they performed on "Soul Train" in 1974. MDLT were your average "one-hit-wonders" kind of group that just didn't have it, if you know what I mean. Papa Joe, the quintessential businessman, took the girls under his wings hoping to make them "stars," but talented they weren't, and MDLT fizzled before they sparked.

During their tour, Joseph Jackson arranged an entire Jackson family show, including the three sisters—Rebbie, LaToya, and Janet, to appear at the famed MGM Grand Hotel in Las Vegas. Their cabaret-style variety show was a huge success for the Jacksons, with sellout shows and standing room only crowds, but most critics would say it was a risky venture. The Las Vegas audiences were not your average teenybopper, J-5 fans; they were a much older, mature, adult crowd, that also enjoyed and respected the Jackson family's lavish stage performance. They welcomed the Jacksons with open arms and embraced their musical talents and fun-loving, family-style show. But the Jacksons were very hesitant about Joseph's decision that could have jeopardized their career. They did not want to risk losing any of their younger fans at the expense of gaining more adult fans, because it was the "young folk" that gave the Jackson Five their worldwide fame, success, and notoriety. They were the ones that bought millions of records, attended sold out concerts, and read all the fan magazines that featured the infamous Jackson brothers. They made the Jackson Five famous and they certainly could not afford to lose any of their young fans that gave them their celebrity status. Joseph's chancing on the Las Vegas cabaret shows proved to be a positive move as the Jacksons were maturing themselves and needed to ease out of their "Bubble gum" music and into a more adult, soulful sound.

As the Jacksons themselves were maturing into young men, they were each displaying their own unique styles and individual personas, identifying themselves to the world. They were also keeping up with the fashion trends of the time, even with their hair styles, as Jermaine and Michael began sporting the newest "perm" style hairdo. This hair style was a trendier look than the natural afro and basically looked like a relaxed afro, but was a lot harder to achieve. Jackson Five fans soon followed the trend and got their hair "permed" also, including me. I forced my two sisters, Jackie and Suzette, to give me a "home perm," since we couldn't always afford to go to a salon to get our hair done. They knew how to work a hot comb like a magic wand and worked their hair magic on me! They put the magic hot comb on top of the stove burner and turned up the fire sky-high, while I sat in the kitchen chair and watched this metal comb get hotter and hotter! I was afraid they were going to burn all of my hair off with that "torch," but they said they knew exactly what they were doing. First, they greased up my entire head with Dixie Peach hair dressing, to protect the hair from burning. Then they took that fiery hot comb and applied it to my young, virgin hair, straightening it out section by section. I was in a state of sheer panic about this point, but they insisted my hair would be just fine. Their finishing touch was to set my hair in hot rollers to lock in the style. When the "magician beauticians" completed their work. I was astounded, amazed, and spellbound... they had performed the impossible! I had the exact same perm style as Jermaine and Michael Jackson and I was steppin'! When I went to school the next day, all my buddies were jealous because the girls were all over me and my new "do." They all had to get the "home perm" special, like me, because they didn't want me to have the chicks to myself! I didn't mind, though because I was flattered by all the attention. Besides, how many girls can one man handle?

TOUCHED BY THE JACKSONS

CHAPTER 6
Childhood

Children are God's little angels from heaven, sent down on this earth to bring love, joy, and happiness to the world. They are innocent, not knowing of evil and sin. Their hearts and minds are pure and their souls are untainted. They are carefree spirits in this existence until evil is thrust upon them and they no longer are 100% pure. They are untarnished, if not physically then spiritually in their souls. Children are precious and should be nurtured, not only by their parents and family members, but by the entire world. They should be enriched by different cultures, nature, the arts, religious faith, their communities in which they reside; everything that touches their lives. I love children and cherish their purity and honesty. I, myself, have always had the carefree spirit of a child and have seen life *"with a child's heart."* I was raised to understand there is evil in this world, but to still be kind and respectful towards others. I always had faith and trust in people, until one day in the summer of 1975. My life was scarred by someone that I trusted.

I wanted to participate in some summertime fun and activities so I joined the local Summer Day Camp, along with some of my (male) friends. We all were recruited by the same camp counselor, a male, to join his Boys Club at the day camp. He was really nice to us and participated in all the games and activities along with us. But it didn't take long for me to see that this counselor always had the young boys in my age group around him all the time. He was a little too nice, a little too friendly, a little too touchy, just a little too much, if you know what I mean. One day, this counselor got a little too close and violated my innocence by touching my genitals and fondling me. I felt completely violated in every which way as I ran like a bat out of hell all the way home. At first, I didn't tell anyone because I was so confused, embarrassed, upset, angry, and afraid no one would believe me. But my family knew immediately that something was wrong because I wasn't myself—I was grouchy, I didn't eat dinner, I didn't listen to my Jackson Five music, I didn't watch any television, I didn't want anything. My mother kept asking me what was wrong and I just kept telling her "nothing," without much conviction. Finally, about 3:00 AM, I went into my mother's room, woke her up, and told her what had happened. She was first angry with me because I didn't tell her right away, but she was more concerned about me and wanted to know in detail what exactly had happened. She started asking me a million questions—"Where did he touch you?" "How many times did he do this to you?" "Did he hurt you in any way?" "Did he penetrate you?" All these questions were coming at me so fast, I was having anxiety and couldn't think straight. And some of her words I couldn't even comprehend because they were too mature for me. All I could say was that he had touched my genital area and parts of my body that made me feel dirty, then I ran the hell out of there and didn't stop until I was home safe. My mother was so disgusted and enraged by the perversion of this man, she called the cops immediately to come to our house so we could press charges against this camp counselor. My father could not understand the demented mentality of this man and having so much hate and anger for him, would have stoned him to death if given the opportunity.

CHILDHOOD

Once the police department began filing my report, we were informed that the man who had fondled me had done this to several other young boys, he had served time in prison a few times for similar sexual charges all involving young boys, and to top it all off, somehow managed to get a job as a counselor despite his previous record of sexual assault and misconduct! *Where is the justice in this world?!* And why does the United States Judicial System allow people who are sick, deranged, psychotic, and dangerous back on the streets when they promise to make our streets and environment a safe haven place, when they are the ones who let this garbage back out in the world. I don't know how this man finagled his way into that job, but it gives me chills to think of all the boys he could have molested, all the ones he did molest and never said anything, and the few brave ones that came forward after my mother had him arrested and charged. Once the nightmare was over and the man was incarcerated again, my family kept a very close eye on me, wouldn't let me out of their sight, and made me feel like a prince, like I was of royalty and they had to protect me. They were being overly cautious of everyone, but can you blame them after such a horrifying ordeal?

It just sickens me to see people in this world that are capable of such hideous acts, especially against children. My heart cries out for children, all children, that are victims of all kinds of abuse and neglect each and every day; sexual abuse, physical abuse, verbal and mental abuse, and parental neglect. How could anyone hurt, or even think of hurting an innocent child? Every form of abuse or neglect is very detrimental to a child because it strips the child of his/her *childhood* and forces the child to think and act as an adult in order to survive. Children are the most precious, most important "things" in this world because they are our future, and they are the *children of the light*. In order for them to run this world when they come of age, they need to be educated, disciplined, loved, and nurtured, not neglected and abused. *You better make a way for the young folks*! If they are raised and treated like savages, then this world will eventually become nothing but a warzone, full of rebellion, hate, revenge, genocide, homicide, suicide, and we the people of the human race, will be to blame for the ending of the world. It makes me think about one of my favorite songs, "If'n I Was God," by Michael Jackson, which tells of all the things he would change in this world if he was God. He tells of how *"nobody would hurt nobody else,"* and how he *"wouldn't set the sun at night, 'til everyone was treated right, by everyone they see."* Such a simple song but so meaningful. It tells you that he would take away all the pain and suffering in this world, all the hurt and hate, all the crime and poverty, if he was God. I often wish I could do the same, as God. But as Michael Jackson said, "I don't try to be God, but I try to be Godlike." And this is what I try to do myself in being Godlike, and that is by praying, giving and loving thy neighbor. But in order for all the people to be Godlike themselves, they must start with the *man in the mirror* and *make that change*, because we all are children of God.

After being exposed to this incident that stripped me of my *childhood* innocence and made me see a side of "adult" life that I never knew existed, I then saw life through an adult's eyes, not a child's eyes. I could no longer wander through life carefree, *with a child's heart*, playing all day long without a worry in the world. I was forced to not trust people anymore, especially adults, until I knew for sure that they were "normal" and wouldn't do anything to harm me physically, mentally, or spiritually. But as time went by and I grew older and wiser, I overcame my scars and my wounds healed. *Sadness had been close as my next of kin... then happy came one day... and chased my blues away.*

  I can understand and sympathize with Michael Jackson when he describes his *childhood* as something he missed, something that was stolen from him, something that he was forced to forget as he worked day after day at being one of the famed Jackson Five. He didn't have time to enjoy a *childhood* because he was too busy working. Although he loved the celebrity status and performing with his brothers, there were many times I'm sure that he wanted to ride his bike and had to practice, wanted to play basketball, but he was in a hotel, wanted to go to an amusement park, but would be mobbed by thousands of fans... frankly, there wasn't a whole lot of time to be a kid. Even some of the places that the Jackson Five performed at struggling to become famous, like strip joints and topless bars, had to affect them in a negative way because it robbed them of seeing life through a child's eyes. They saw things that weren't meant for a child to see as their *childhood* innocence was being chipped away, piece by piece, in the process. But I guess, in a way, it helped to prepare them for the trials and tribulations of life as celebrities and as men, and kept them a step ahead of the game.

TOUCHED BY THE JACKSONS

CHAPTER 7
Forever Came Today

The summer of '75 brings back memories of backyard bar-b-ques and neighborhood block parties with everyone just getting together to enjoy some good food, have a little drink, chat with some friends, and dance to the latest music! Some folks had their music blasting so loud, you could hear it from blocks away! But what I remember most is all the ladies dancing, swinging their butts back and forth to the sounds of the Jacksons' song "Body Language," singing the lyrics "Shake it to the east, shake it to the west, shake it to the girl, the one you love best." And they were shaking it all right! They shook it so much that the men played that song over and over and over, just to watch all the women dance and shake their booties! "Body Language" was one of the hit songs from the Jackson Five's *Moving Violations* album, along with the title cut, "Moving Violations," "Forever Came Today," and "All I Do Is Think Of You," the romantic ballad from the album. "Forever Came Today" was the biggest hit single off the *Moving Violations* album, and was the last single the Jackson Five released for Motown Records, as well as the last album.

The Jackson brothers, along with their manager/father, Joseph Jackson, were experiencing some "irreconcilable differences" with Motown Records and decided not to renew their contract with Motown at the end of its term. Even though the Jackson Five, the golden protégés of Motown, had tremendous worldwide success with the schooling of Berry

Gordy and Motown Records, Joseph Jackson and his sons felt that they could demand a higher royalty because of their sales and it was time for the brothers to have more artistic freedom with their music. They felt that they should be given the opportunity to expand their talents into writing and producing their own songs and Motown did not want to grant them that freedom. Motown felt it was too risky and still wanted control over all the music the Jackson Five recorded. Joseph Jackson struck a desirable deal with CBS/Epic Records which promised the Jackson brothers more artistic freedom than Motown had ever allowed, and upon expiration of their contract with Motown in the spring of 1976, the Jacksons would make their move to Epic Records. But there was one small problem; brother Jermaine, who was married to Motown president Berry Gordy's daughter Hazel, felt very loyal to Motown Records and his wife, and *"forever came today"* when he chose to remain with Motown as a solo artist while his brothers signed with Epic Records. It was one of the most difficult decisions Jermaine has ever had to make in his life because it affected his family and his wife's family, no matter what his choice would be. Luckily, everyone supported Jermaine in his decision and even though his brothers would miss him as part of the group, they were still his family and respected his choice.

    The official announcement was made by Joe Jackson at a press conference in New York City, but the split from Motown wasn't a smooth and easy one. There were a few legal matters that needed to be settled first, such as the name of the group, the "Jackson Five," and their logo, were registered and owned by Motown, and therefore could no longer be used by the Jackson brothers once they left the company. The group then had to legally become "The Jacksons" on Epic Records. But according to their contract with Motown, the Jackson Five still owed the record company another album before the date of expiration, and Joseph refused to comply, forcing Motown Records to file depositions against the Jacksons seeking over twenty-million dollars in damages. The lawsuit was finally settled some five years down the line without much hoopla, as the Jacksons' career with CBS/Epic Records soared to new heights.

    The Jacksons, knowing that the show must go on, had to perform for the first time on television without brother Jermaine on "The Mike Douglas Show," live in Las Vegas. It was so strange and kind of sad to see the Jacksons on-stage without Jermaine at Michael's left, playing bass guitar, taking the lead vocals here and there. Anyone watching the Jacksons minus their brother could see they obviously missed him on that stage and were a little down about his absence. Although they tried to mask their sadness, it was written all over their faces. Even I felt emotional about it like Jermaine was my own brother, especially coming from a large family, just like the Jacksons, I know what it feels like when one of my siblings isn't there for a holiday or birthday party... everyone goes on with the celebration, but deep down they're missing that person dearly. It was still business as usual as the Jacksons were promoting their *Moving Violations* album on Motown Records, released in 1975, the same time Michael was promoting his solo album also on Motown, *Forever Michael*. The biggest hits off the album, *Forever Michael*, were "One Day In Your Life," "We're Almost There," and "Just A Little Bit Of You." *Forever Michael* wasn't as successful as his previous solo albums, perhaps because Michael was maturing and so was the music that he and his brothers were doing this year. Also, Michael had certainly entered the pubescent time of his life and his voice was noticeably changing. He could no longer hit those very high notes he once could and his voice would sometimes, unavoidably crack, no matter how hard he tried to prevent it. But more importantly, the Jacksons were going through a transition in their career as their musical style was changing and they were attracting more adult fans while their "Bubble gum" fans either grew with them or chose not to. Either way, the Jacksons didn't lose any momentum in their career as they crossed yet another road to success.

That same summer (of '75), there was a concert tour featuring several Black Soul and R & B artists, such as Chaka Khan and Earth Wind & Fire, that was traveling around city to city throughout the summer, just like the classic Budweiser Superfest concert series (it may have even been a part of the Superfest series—I just don't remember!), and it was scheduled to come to Shea Stadium, in Queens, NY. Still to this day, I don't remember who the other artists appearing at the concert were, but the featured performers at Shea Stadium were the Jackson Five! The Jackson family was still going back and forth to Las Vegas for their "Jackson Family Revue" while they were touring the country at the same time! I was only 11 years old at the time and too young to go to a concert by myself, so I had to beg and plead with my mother to let me go. She was afraid some crazed, fanatical fans would stomp all over me or hurt me trying to get close to the Jacksons, or feared I would just get lost in the crowd. But finally she gave in and allowed me to go, under the condition that one of my older siblings had to go with me to act as my chaperon. Fine with me! As long as I get to see the Jacksons live and in concert, I don't care if my grandmother comes with me! Knowing how strongly I wanted to see the Jacksons, my mother took some of her rent money out to pay for my ticket to the concert. But then, as *"destiny"* would have it, all my hard work of begging, crying, pleading, sweet-talking, and stomping, was done in vain because the entire concert got canceled. For security reasons, the one and only Jackson Five concert in the New York City area that year got canceled because of riots at previous other concerts at Shea Stadium. It was a time of mourning for me as my dream of a lifetime got crushed, literally, by riots! Now that I think about it, with the fame and popularity of the Jackson Five, the concert at Shea Stadium would have been wild, exciting, and chaotic, and probably even *dangerous* without the proper security. But it certainly would have been bigger than the Beatles concert at Shea Stadium by far!

CHAPTER 8
Destiny

Another daring career move by the Jacksons spawned their first weekly television variety show on CBS, appropriately titled "The Jacksons." Their family-oriented variety show featured the entire Jackson clan, including the three sisters, Rebbie, LaToya, and Janet. Truthfully, it was the first time the public really got a chance to see the Jackson sisters perform with their brothers on television, except for the Jackson family revues in Las Vegas, which obviously were not televised. This summertime TV series was a huge success for the Jacksons, especially since variety shows in the 70's were like talk shows in the 90's. I was overwhelmingly *happy* that the Jacksons finally had their own weekly television series, instead of just a TV special here and there; I could tune in once a week and get my shot of "Jackson juice" to keep me going all week! But I've come to learn through years of experience in this business that when your are such a big superstar, being on a weekly show can sometimes do more damage than good to your career. Michael Jackson himself even said this—when you "flood the market" and over saturate yourself to the public, people get tired of you real fast. All over America, people are watching you come into their living rooms week after week, the thrill and excitement are gone, and then it becomes *overkill*. Just look at "The Donny & Marie (Osmond) Show," also of the 70's. Their show lasted on the air much longer than it should have and actually became annoying to see them after a while, on television every Friday night. Music was changing as the Disco era emerged and Donny and Marie were still singing "I'm a little bit country... I'm a little bit rock 'n roll!" Variety shows were basically dead by this time and so was their musical style. Whatever little talent they did have was no longer working for them and by letting their show's longevity run into "sudden death," it killed their careers along with it. I'm so glad the Jacksons did not pursue the same overextended TV career as Donny and Marie because even though their talent surpasses the Osmonds by far, it may have still scarred their careers.

Many celebrities today that once had their own television variety show and are no longer at the peak of their career have resorted to performing at their own theater in a place called Branson, Missouri. These performers, who shall remain nameless, could no longer sellout any large scale venues and in order to keep working, had to buy their own theater to book their own shows in hopes that whatever loyal fans they have would come to see them at their own theater. But how long will your fans keep coming to see you when your little "fan club" has diminished over the years? These performers that are still holding on to yesterday, to whatever "was" in their career, are nothing but has-beens. Especially the Osmonds—they are the has-beens that never was, and the wannabe's that never will! This oasis in the heart of the Midwest is like the "Island of Misfit Toys," and the artists performing there are like the toys that nobody wants. It's pathetic—even the way Branson only caters to "White" America is a joke. Believe me, you won't find too many people of color in that town! They're over in St. Louis, checking out the cool Jazz scene and the red-hot Blues!

I'm sure Motown was crying the blues at the loss of their most successful, most profitable group that made millions for them. Since the J5 did not fulfill their contract with Motown and give them the last album, the head honchos of Motown decided to release a Jackson Five album of previously recorded music and purposely release it before the Jacksons new album for CBS/Epic Records debuted. *Joyful Jukebox Music* was released by Motown with much disappointment as it didn't even enter the top 100 albums chart. It was an immature move by Motown—sort of a slap in the face hoping to knock down the possibility of a successful first album for their new record company. But such antics proved to be nothing but a slap back as the Jacksons released their first single, "Enjoy Yourself," from their debut album for CBS/Epic Records entitled *The Jacksons*. This album exploded like a bomb to the top of the charts and outsold the last few albums for Motown by far! Other hit singles from the album were "Show You The Way To Go," "Think Happy," and "Keep On Dancin'." The Jackson brothers were certainly *"enjoying"* themselves as their move to CBS/Epic proved to be the right one.

But rumor had it that the Jacksons would never reunite with brother Jermaine again since he decided to remain at Motown. The press had a field day with all the gossip and rumors, speculating the entire group would break up and all sorts of ridiculous things, but I knew in my heart the brothers wouldn't allow that to happen. I remember the impact of Jermaine leaving his brothers to pursue his solo career left a lot of loyal fans hurt and sad, but I was hopeful and optimistic that one day all the brothers would reunite on-stage once again. It was 4 years later, in 1979, that Jermaine made his 1st Jackson family stage appearance with all his brothers; Tito, Marlon, Jackie, Michael, and Randy, on "The Midnight Special" TV show, hosted by the Jackson brothers themselves. Jermaine joined his brothers to sing the title cut of their current album release—*Destiny*. And what a joyous *destiny* it was to see Jermaine performing with his brothers in unity and the magic of the Jackson family together again. The magic never died, it just rekindled itself at the next Jackson family reunion... on the "Motown's 25th Anniversary...Yesterday, Today, Forever" television special. This wonderful anniversary celebration for Motown Records featured many of its renowned artists, but the climactic moment of the evening came when the Jackson brothers took center stage. Everyone watching all around the world was spellbound by the magic of the Jacksons. There was so much love, happiness, and unity generating from their performance on stage that you could feel the warmth of their presence whether you were right there in the same auditorium or home watching them on television. The feeling was so beautiful and so strong like it was the rebirth of the Jackson Five all over again. It was an experience that most watching will never forget.

Just like the New York City Blackout of '77 on July 11, 1977—who, from New York, could forget that? The summer of '77 was as hot as hell man, and people had no choice but to turn on those fans and air conditioners to keep cool. Even most fire hydrants in the neighborhood were opened for people to get cooled off by the water. Everyone running their fans and air conditioners constantly during the dreadful heat wave caused the city's electric generators to be forced into maximum overdrive and knocked out the electric power throughout the majority of New York City and its 5 boroughs. I have never seen so much mayhem and chaos—people were running through the streets, looting, robbing, breaking windows—it was really scary! But to me, the worst part about the whole ordeal was that I couldn't listen to my Jackson music for 2 or 3 days! This was the longest I ever went without my Jackson music and I felt like I was going through withdrawal, like a junkie! It was horrible... I felt like I was in a bad "Twilight Zone" episode that wouldn't end! But finally, when power was restored, I played my Jackson music nonstop for hours! I had to make up for lost time, you know.

But time certainly wasn't lost as "The Jacksons" television variety show returned by popular demand for yet another season, and even ran longer than the last season. Their show came on Wednesday nights in New York and kicked "The Bionic Woman" in the ass, who was running in the same time slot! The Jacksons were still busy promoting their first album for CBS/Epic Records and touring Europe, when they were honored with an invitation to perform for Queen Elizabeth of England at a Royal Command Performance. I say, these young boys from Gary, Indiana were hobnobbing with royalty! What an accomplishment it was for the Jackson brothers to receive a royal invitation from the Queen herself! It's not every day that the Queen personally invites someone to perform for Her Royal Highness and family.

As the Jacksons adjusted to their new-found freedom artistically, Michael Jackson expanded his talents into acting, as he was chosen to play the Scarecrow in the film, *The Wiz*. This Black film adaptation of the Broadway hit musical of the same name, featured an all-star line-up of costars, including Diana Ross, Richard Pryor, and Ted Ross, with world-renowned music producer and arranger, Quincy Jones, heading the project. This was a **BIG** first for Michael—1. the first time Michael ever starred in a major motion picture, 2. the first time Michael ever lived away from his family for a long length of time, even though sister LaToya stayed with him in New York throughout the filming schedule, 3. the first time Michael ever had to really transform into a character, the Scarecrow, with all the heavy theatrical make-up and costumes he had to wear everyday during filming, and 4. the first time Michael ever worked with Quincy Jones (and we all know it certainly wasn't his last). It was an experience that Michael slates as being one of the greatest in his life. It's just too bad that the film got unfavorable reviews from American film critics which contributed to the lagging tickets sales. Ironically, Michael himself was praised for his role of the Scarecrow, which seemed tailor-made for him, in the film that was not well-suited for the public's interest.

CHAPTER 9
Goin' Places

The Jacksons were definitely *Goin' Places* with their second album release on Epic Records. Although the album spawned 6 radio hits for the Jacksons, its overall sales did not score any home runs for them. Under most circumstances, this would not have been a problem for any artist and their record company, but since this was the world-famous Jacksons' second album with a new record label, it was not an impressive follow-up to their debut album for Epic. The radio hits off the album were the title cut, "Goin' Places," "Even Though You're Gone," "Music's Takin' Over," "Jump For Joy," "Find Me A Girl," and "Different Kind of Lady," which was written and produced by the Jacksons. The Jacksons launched a world concert tour for this album in January 1978, and during their hectic tour schedule, managed to record their next album for Epic Records. The Jackson brothers knew what they were capable of creatively and needed the opportunity to prove it to their record company and the public that they could write and produce their own smash album. Well, opportunity finally came a' knockin' when the President of Epic Records granted them the chance they've been waiting for—the chance to write and produce their third album for Epic... the chance to prove their *Destiny*.

Music was again evolving as people everywhere caught the *Saturday Night Fever* and were doing the hustle to their favorite disco beat! Even my own mother and father were burning up the dance floor every weekend, trying to revitalize their youth, sporting the embarrassing polyester "disco" ensemble. I can't believe even my father wore all those gold chains with an opened, button-down disco shirt, trying to look so cool. He thought he was *profilin'* and *stylin'*! But what was it about disco music that made everyone flock to the discotheques, boogie all night long, regardless of how young or mainly, how old they were? The young ones I can understand, but the old folks, acting like they were in their twenties again, how and why did disco music affect them in such a way? It's like a mystery of the unknown; we may never know the answer. And despite all those non-disco goers, displaying their "Disco Sucks" bumper stickers and T-shirts, disco music made its mark on music *history*, and also revolutionized the nightclub scene that has been preserved in American pop culture.

  Keeping with the music trends of the time, the Jacksons released their 1st single from their third album on Epic entitled, "Blame It On The Boogie," a disco hit that topped the charts for them. The Jacksons were influenced by the popular disco music of the time and incorporated that sound with their own, unique "Jackson-esque" music, creating the Jackson sound that clearly identifies them musically in the industry. The Jacksons' third album on Epic Records, *Destiny*, reveals THE Jackson sound they created that integrated the Disco sound with R & B, Pop, and Soul, into that distinctive Jackson sound, recognizable throughout the world. Much unlike the "Bubble gum" years at Motown, the "Philadelphia" sound of their last 2 albums weaned them out of that adolescent, teenybopper music geared toward the young teen-agers, and focused on a much more adult audience. Still today you can hear music from old and new artists mimicking and using the signature Jackson sounds in their music. Well, you know the old saying... imitation is the best form of flattery!

The next hit from *Destiny* soon followed; "Shake Your Body (Down To The Ground)," another chart-busting disco hit for the Jacksons. The Jacksons promoted "Blame It On The Boogie" by releasing a music video of the song, which boosted the sales and success of the single. But their powerful dance hit, "Shake Your Body (Down To The Ground)" was the song that became their first multi-platinum single and biggest selling single, selling over three million copies. It was definitely their biggest kick-ass concert song that always tore the place out! The overall sales figures and chart numbers spelled s-u-c-c-e-s-s for the Jacksons, but what made everything sublime was that the Jacksons had total control of writing and producing their most successful album to date. It earned them the respect in the industry as being not only great singers, but also accomplished songwriters and producers. The Jacksons' Destiny World Tour, which included the U.S., Europe, Africa, and beyond, was a major force behind the success of the album.

Since the Jacksons were maturing musically and physically and were no longer focusing on the pubescent, "Bubble gum" fans, it was time to change their "Bubble gum" afros into the hair style of the future... the *jheri curl*! One by one, the Jackson brothers entered the "world of curls" while I decided to stay an "afro-disiac." But I couldn't keep living in yesteryear for long with my footlong afro and decided to do the cultural thing and do my hair in cornrows, like Stevie Wonder. Every week I had to have my hair re-braided in different styles, 'cause it was cool. But that shit would really hurt sometimes! Pulling out the braids, combing the knots out, shampooing the hair, pulling the hair tightly into new braids... man, anyone who's been through that can tell you I'm not lying, it hurts! After a few years of "braid trauma" to the head, I finally gave in and decided to cut Sampson's locks off. It was time for that Jackson-jheri curl look! I took out my afro comb, untangled all my braids, got that afro pick and picked my hair out to **THERE**!! **BOOM**! As I walked down Fulton Street to the salon, I felt a little Superfly-ish as the wind blew through my J5 do! When I walked into the salon with my big-ass 'fro, the owner wasted no time in getting me into her chair! Abracadabra, alacazam... five hours later, I was a *Jheri Curl Man*!

CHAPTER 10
Girlfriend

As I sat in homeroom class the first day of Junior High School, in walked the angel of my eyes. She was a vision of loveliness; a striking beauty that captures you from afar. When she came walking in the classroom that day, I wanted that sweet flower for my garden! I felt like I was in a scene from the Disney motion picture *Bambi*, where it's springtime and Bambi and his pals have become adolescents and get spring fever when all the little female "flowers" walk by and flirt with them. They become captivated and entranced as they are smitten by love and spring fever! Well here I was doing the same thing, with my nose wide open for my sweet thing, Mona. She was my first real steady girlfriend and *my first one*, if you know what I mean. I would sometimes ride my bike to school, but sometimes, when the fever hit me, I would take a detour and head straight to Mona's house and cut school with her. I would jump on my bike, and begin pumping feverishly, like the old, nasty lady from *The Wizard of Oz*, while the theme music played in my head, "*Dun da dun da da da, dun da dun da da da...*" We would spend all day playing "house" together and one thing led to another and... it happened. I was no longer an innocent little boy; I lost my virginity at a young age and thought I was all that. Mona was a little fast and very persistent, considering that we were only 14 years old at the time. My house calls started to become a weekly rendezvous, until the school finally picked up on it and sent home letters to our parents. Of course we both lied and told our parents we were with only our friends... "you know Ma, me and the fellas." But we were getting too greedy, spending too much time together, when one day we almost got caught by her mother. She unexpectedly came home from work early that day and Mona and I were upstairs in her room fooling around. All of a sudden, we heard a knock on her bedroom door and jumped up like leapfrogs and sprang towards the door. I think it was obvious to her mother what was going on, but I turned on the sweet, puppy dog eyes and the charm so we wouldn't get in any trouble. The master plan worked (thank God!), but Mona and I were a lot more careful from then on. But you know how "puppy love" is, it doesn't last forever. So it was time to move on to the next flower.

My father lived in a studio apartment in a beautiful brownstone on Vanderbilt Avenue in Brooklyn, upstairs from Miss Grant and her granddaughter, Malka. Miss Grant was a wonderful lady that did everything in the best interest of Malka, but was also very strict with her, too. Malka went to a private school and always wore the nicest clothes and had her hair done like she was going to church every day. I started going to my father's house when I was 15 to pick up my weekly allowance of $25 (not bad, huh) and this is how Malka and I began dating. Malka is a long-time friend of my family's; her mother, Jackie, and my eldest siblings used to hang out together and party, so she was no stranger to the family. Her mother had her at a very young age because she was living life in the fast lane and didn't know how to slow down. Unfortunately, she came to a sudden stop when she died, due to her "experimenting," and Malka was left in the care of her grandmother.

I guess my father really liked Malka and sort of felt sorry

for her, because she didn't have any parents, only Miss Grant, and he treated her like one of his daughters. He would often bail her out when she came home late on a school night and throw pebbles at his window to get him to come down to unlock the front door and bring her up to his apartment. He would lie and tell her grandmother that she was home the whole time with him doing her homework, so she wouldn't get punished. But as much as he liked her, my father tried to discourage me from dating Malka because he felt she might follow in the same footsteps her own mother did, and would hurt me in the end. He just didn't feel that Malka was the right one for me. But I was just like your average teen-ager that doesn't want to listen and feels what they do and say is right, not realizing that their parents have been in their shoes already, and disregarded his advice and rebelled against him.

    Malka and I swore we were "in love" and moved a little too fast with our relationship because in just a few months, she became pregnant. Before it could really sink in that I was about to become a father, hands were coming at me left and right from friends and family congratulating me. But my father didn't say anything at first: he wanted to sit me down for our first "man to man" talk. His first words were, and I quote, "Congratulations Arthur." I asked him why was he calling me Arthur, since his "pet" name for me was Boy. He never called me by my given name, Arthur, which was his father's name, my grandfather's name, so I knew he meant business. "First things first, your allowance has been stopped. And you have to get a job. I'm not going to call you Boy anymore, I'm going to call you Arthur (even though he sometimes slipped and called me Boy, which I preferred anyway). Be a man and take care of your responsibilities." I took heed to his words as I juggled high school with some part-time jobs, trying to fend for myself and save money for the baby on the way. I did the usual paper routes, fast food restaurants, factory work, etc., because I had to be the man.

When my first son was born, I was so proud of him, looking at something that I had created. But at the hospital, since I was only 16 and looked even younger, I sometimes had a problem getting in to the Maternity Ward, because they thought I was a kid myself. Then it became a big joke among all the nurses in the ward that I was such a young looking guy, I didn't look old enough to be a father. On the 4th of July 1980, my first son, Timothy LaShawn, was born, just before the big fireworks celebration! We named him Timothy, which is my middle name that I gave myself, literally, because I was a big fan of the "Lassie" TV show and I wanted to be like the boy Timmy on the show. I would pretend my dog Bebe was Lassie and try to make her act out the shows with me like we were Timmy and Lassie, but unfortunately, Bebe wasn't a trained dog like Lassie and would only let me torment her for about 5 minutes before running out of the room. I wanted to be Timmy and used to tell everyone, even strangers "Call me Timmy, call me Timmy! My name's not Arthur!" For the longest time I wouldn't even answer to anyone that called me anything but Timmy... really! I was a total brat! I kept asking my mother to change my name to Timmy; I didn't want to be Arthur anymore. And with enough annoying persistence, I coerced my mother into legally giving me the name Timothy, even if it was my middle name. Mind you, I was only five years old at the time and was slick enough to make my mother legally change my name through the courts and everything, because I wanted to be Timmy! Unbelievable! Everyone in my family still laughs about it to this day, because they couldn't believe how far I went to get the name Timothy!

Then just as I was beginning to adapt to the daily life and routine of fatherhood; bottles, diapers, sleep deprivation, 2 months later Malka tells me she's pregnant again. **WHAT?!** How could that happen? What were we thinking? It couldn't happen again, not that quickly. Surprise, surprise, yes it can! Everyone in my family and hers shook their heads in shame because we should have known better. Bad enough we just had a baby, but we were babies ourselves—Malka was 18 and I was 16. I even got really mad at myself and at her for being so careless. But what good did that do me; it wasn't going to solve anything, only make matters worse. I soon got over myself and started preparing for baby #2 already on the way.

Timothy was a very *happy* baby, always laughing and smiling for no apparent reason. He made the strain of everything a lot easier to deal with since he was such a good baby. I felt bad because I wasn't there when Timothy was born and really wanted to be, but when Malka went into labor, she was out with some of her family that day and by the time they got her to the hospital and they called me, it was too late when I arrived. Timothy was already born. But this time we promised each other we wouldn't let that happen again so I could be there with her for the second birth.

As promised, Malka called me about 6:00 AM on June 13, 1981 and said "This is it! Hurry over here!" I got up and ran all the way to her house in Fort Greene—quite a distance from my house on Putnam Avenue in Bedford-Stuyvesant—and I didn't stop until I reached the front steps of her house on Vanderbilt Avenue. As I got within a block or so from her house, I could hear screams drifting through the air like a scene from a horror movie, just wafting through the quiet early morning street. When I got there, she was on the floor writhing in severe pain and I completely panicked! I went to get one of her neighbors to help me stop a taxi cab (or "gypsy" cab as we call 'em in the 'hood) to rush her to the hospital on time. We ran up and down Fulton Street trying to get somebody, anybody, to take us to the hospital! And the few cab drivers that actually did stop for us, wouldn't take us because they didn't want a mess in their back seat! We had already called the ambulance and they still hadn't arrived, and Malka's contractions were coming closer and closer together! Fear was written all over my face because I wanted to be there for the birth, but I didn't want to be the one making the delivery! Finally, the paramedics arrived, but they were too late; Malka was already having the baby on the floor. We were running around screaming, "Boil water! Get some sheets!," not knowing what else to do. What the hell are we boiling water for anyway? It's gonna be too hot to use! Within minutes, I saw my second son, Arthur Gemaile, being born right before my eyes. He came into the world with an audience watching him—2 paramedics, 2 policemen, Miss Grant, her neighbor, me and little Timmy, who witnessed the whole thing, and he was just turning a year old. It was such a beautiful event, I wish I had a video camera to record every minute of it. There's nothing more beautiful than witnessing the birth of a child you created with your "love wife" and watching them come into the world. Even though I was young, it seemed like all the meanings of life were revealed to me. I felt like Moses walking up that mountain, looking for the answers to life and finding out what life is all about and what is has to offer.

Everyone's faces in the room lit up with happiness after witnessing such a miraculous moment. One policeman told me he wished he could have experienced his wife giving birth, but for whatever reason, he wasn't there with her. And here I was, 17 years old, and I had the experience of a lifetime that he didn't have. Immediately after my son was born, I was the first to hold him, and as quickly as they gave him to me, I was overcome by the thrill of the moment, and gave him right back... and ran! I headed straight for the bathroom and relieved myself in every which way possible! My stomach is very weak and couldn't handle all the excitement. I had the paramedic guys knocking on the bathroom door, asking if I was okay in there and making sure I was all right! Once I calmed down and felt better, I came out to hold little Gemaile again. One of the paramedics told us it was the first baby he ever helped to deliver and was so *happy* and proud that Malka's delivery went so well.

We all went back to the same hospital again and the same nurses from last year remembered me and teased me again for being such a young-looking father. They were really nice to us and took extra special care of Gemaile and Malka. I told them they wouldn't see me in there again for a very long time—at least not the maternity ward! No more kids for me! Gemaile cried and cried because he was colicky, and all you could do was walk him, rock him, and sing to him, hoping he would stop crying. Believe me, I wasn't going to let myself have another kid anytime soon, not after hearing all the noise Gemaile made, screaming and crying. That was the biggest wake up call I ever heard!

While the Jacksons were still on their Destiny World Tour, they began recording their next album, not wasting a moment of free time they had. Yet, at the same time, Michael was recording his first solo album for Epic to be released in August of '79. Michael's artistic achievement, *Off The Wall*, which was produced by the legendary Quincy Jones, was a blockbuster hit for Michael. It was a beautiful montage of R & B, Rock, Jazz, and Pop and wonderful display of Michael's coming of age musically, especially as a solo artist. Even the album cover itself with Michael posing in front of a brick wall, wearing a black tuxedo, bow tie, and white sequined socks gleaming from under his too-short tuxedo pants, was a clear statement of his matured, individual style. The album surpassed all expectations as it broke industry records by being the first album in the U.S. with 4 Top Ten singles, 2 of which were number 1 hits, and become certified Gold. And in England, a record 5 hit singles were released from the same album, including the song, "Girlfriend," written by Paul McCartney. The other chart-topping hits off the album were "Don't Stop 'Til You Get Enough," "Rock With You," "Working Day And Night," and "She's Out Of My Life." *Off The Wall* remained on both the Pop and Black charts for months, and its impressive sales figures brought it to Gold and Platinum status. *Life ain't so bad at all!*

CHAPTER 11
Triumph

Most artists create only one masterpiece in their lifetime, and the Jacksons' true masterpiece was their 1980 *Triumph* album. The music alone on this album was so outstanding, as it captured the heart and soul of each and every one of the Jacksons. You could really listen and identify the individual sounds that were created by the Jackson brothers and how they all merged together to form *Triumph*. From the time they left Motown, the Jacksons' individual musical styles were developing rapidly as they had more and more opportunity to express themselves creatively, as a unit and also as individual performers.

Oldest brother Jackie is the strength of the group and the main harmonizer. His smooth, falsetto harmonies and vocal arrangements are distinguished in every Jackson song. Jackie is also the most athletic, excelling in many sports, especially baseball. His velvety-smooth vocals, perfectly chiseled body, and sculptured face capture your attention like a magnet, especially when he wears his chest-bearing shirts to reveal his Adonis-like body. Women just go crazy over him!

Brother Tito, definitely the most well-known Jackson by name, is the Jacksons' lead guitarist. Tito has lent his self-created guitar riffs to many a Jackson song, adding his spice to the Jackson sound. He is the most laid-back brother that really loves playing his music, but certainly doesn't do it for the celebrity of it. Tito is your average "family man" that loves to work on cars and spend time at home out of the limelight. He is very family oriented and his brothers hold the utmost respect for him.

Brother Marlon, the "dancingest Jackson," adds his style of funk to the Jacksons' music. Marlon acts as Michael's shadow on stage, filling in the gaps at center stage when Michael steps back. He's a powerful performer and knows how to take control of the stage, always giving 110% and then some. Marlon is also very charming and personable, like a best friend, which has won him the hearts of millions of fans.

Randy, the youngest Jackson brother, proved himself as a Jackson by watching and learning from his older brothers as he was coming up. The quiet little shy guy showed us all a thing or two as he became the most creative musician out of all the Jackson brothers. He still remains one of the driving forces behind the unique sound of the Jacksons, with his talents spanning into playing several instruments, writing, arranging, and producing. Randy's outstanding creativity brings the Jacksons' music to life.

Michael Jackson's presence alone could blow you out of your seat. He is unparalleled as a performer and explodes every time he hits the stage. Michael is also a perfectionist and will not settle for second best. As the lead singer, Michael's melodic vocals and unique ad-libs and vocalized background sounds, are the heartfelt soul of the Jacksons' music. His finesse and unique dance style, along with artistic input from brothers Jackie and Marlon, have created the most powerful dance routines that the Jacksons have become famous for. Yet he still has that boyish charm with big, brown eyes and a captivating smile that melts your heart.

Brother Jermaine, the romantic balladeer, was the first Black teen idol in America, with his striking good looks and smooth R & B vocals. His soulful, melodic voice is like the icing on the cake in every Jackson song. Jermaine is also the bass guitar player of the group and thumps and plucks that bass, adding his own groove and funk to the sound. He has held his own as a successful solo artist since his departure from the group in 1976, and remains a positive force behind the Jackson brothers' music.

The force behind the *Triumph* album was the music itself. Musically, the album was orchestrated like a full symphony, complete with percussion, string, and wind sections, along with the Jacksons' vocals. Their sound was innovative, brilliant, exciting, unique… and they had created it all themselves. Creatively, they had reached their highest plateau with *Triumph*. The biggest hits from the album were "Heartbreak Hotel," "Can You Feel It," "Lovely One," and "Walk Right Now." This album is one of my all-time favorite albums and believe it or not, got played so much that I wore out the grooves on the record and lost most of the sound quality! I actually had to buy another copy so I could continue listening to it!

Along with the album, the Jacksons released another work of art, *The Triumph* (short film), a music video for the single "Can You Feel It." The Jacksons as creators and producers, have demonstrated their ingenious capabilities with this outstanding presentation. The concept of the Jacksons' short film was so imaginative, especially at a time when the concept of music videos themselves were just starting to catch on to the public, it was truly a decade ahead of its time and a phenomenal achievement for the Jacksons. This 10 minute long video was so spectacular with technologically advanced special effects that had never been seen before, but focuses on a deeper message for humanity—to spread peace, love, and harmony. The symbolism in the video, the peacock, which is also on the back cover of *Triumph*, represents the beauty in all colors and races uniting together to become one, from the power of music and love. It is an idealistic concept for modern society, but certainly one we should take heed to. The experience of seeing this video in all its wonderment cannot be described in words.

The Jacksons' Triumph World Tour hit the concert scene like an atom bomb in 1981. It was touted as one of the greatest live performances of its time by many a writer and publication. To me, it was **THE** concert of all live concerts! I saw them perform at Madison Square Garden in New York City and I swear, it was the most exciting, live performance I have ever seen in my life! And one thing that I must say was so wonderful about it was that the Jacksons' audience was the most integrated group of people I've ever seen at a concert. It was such a beautiful sight to see, so many faces of different cultures, people just coming together to rejoice in the music of the Jacksons. We, the people, were all the beautiful colors of the rainbow, and the Jacksons were the pot of gold shining at the end of the rainbow. Nothing in this world can bring so many different people together like the power of music and I was so glad to be a part of what the Jacksons had achieved from their music. I felt like I was a part of *history* in the makings! Inside that arena, I looked around and felt so much joy, happiness, and love, it was a spiritual feeling of mankind.

The concert opened with *The Triumph* (short film) before the Jacksons made their appearance on stage. As the entire arena witnessed this historical moment, we all fell under the spell of the Jacksons' music, and rejoiced in our feelings of unity, togetherness, and love. During the scene in the video where the Jacksons were spreading stardust from the heavens down to the earth, everyone joined hands with one another in a chain reaction. It was phenomenal! When the film had finished, the impact it made was so incredible, everyone just stood there in awe and remained silent. They were so moved and speechless by this powerful piece of artwork they had just seen and experienced.

Brother Randy made the first appearance on stage, adorned in a Medieval suit of armor, carrying a glowing torch of fire, symbolizing their *triumph*, and the magical power of the Jacksons' music. He then shouted to the anxiously awaiting crowd "**CAN YOU FEEL IIITTTT??!!!**" His thunderous voice echoed throughout the Garden, giving everyone the feeling of elation because the Jacksons were finally HERE!! Then the remaining Jacksons—Michael, Marlon, Tito, and Jackie—made their grand entrance, arising from beneath the stage. As they made their dramatic ascension from under the stage on a rising platform, the multiple high powered lights followed behind them, then up and over their heads, shining light upon them. They stood motionless, like statues of worship, and the bright lights all around the stage produced an angelic glow around the Jacksons, giving them a Godlike presence. Even their rhinestone-studded costumes reflected all the colorful lights and special effects like a prism. It was breathtaking.

The crowd roared, chanting and stomping their feet like a stampede of elephants, and the mighty Jacksons broke into their opening number "Can You Feel It!" From that moment on, the intensity grew stronger and stronger with each and every song. The Jacksons' performed an integrated blend of their hits from the *Triumph* album back to a medley of their most popular "Bubble gum" hits including "I Want You Back," "ABC," "The Love You Save," and "I'll Be There." They also featured a number of songs from Michael's solo album, *Off The Wall*, since the success of the album was still going strong. The Jacksons' performance was so outstanding it never ceased to amaze me as their energy level never dropped for even a second. They maintained the same explosive energy from the first song to the finale.

After the Jacksons left the stage, the audience went wild, screaming for an encore! Everyone in the audience was shouting in unison "We want more! We want more!" Finally, the Jacksons came running back onto the stage for their 1st encore, Michael's hit song "Working Day & Night." During the song, Michael and his brothers executed a grand illusion, with Michael disappearing and then reappearing at the opposite side of the stage in a cloud of smoke and exploding pyrotechnics. This was the ultimate climax of the show, but the excitement didn't stop there! When Michael reappeared, the Jacksons jumped right into his #1 multi-million selling hit single, "Don't Stop 'Til You Get Enough," with Michael wearing his trademark black tuxedo, bow tie, and his eternally famous, sparkling white sequined socks. This of course, was the outfit made famous on the cover of Michael's 1979 hit solo album, *Off The Wall*.

The last and final song of the show was the smash hit, "Shake Your Body (Down To The Ground)" and by this point, everyone was dancing up and down the aisles like it was a celebrated ritual! Even the security guards couldn't control themselves—they were all dancing, too! This was the song that really took the house down! I was waiting for all the walls to start caving in on us and the roof to start crumbling down! The excitement level had reached its boiling point when the Jacksons had to bring us down out of our frenzy for the closing of the show. As they left the stage, this time for good, everyone stood spellbound by this amazing display of love, unity, and talent that the Jackson brothers gave to their fans. They gave it their all and them some and certainly touched the lives and souls of every person in that arena. It was most definitely a *triumph*!

TOUCHED BY THE JACKSONS

CHAPTER 12
Forever Michael

Not long after the last date of the Triumph World Tour, Michael Jackson was back in the studio working on his follow-up album to *Off The Wall*, again collaborating with Quincy Jones. The Jacksons' success was soaring to levels higher than ever before as they reached the ultimate peak in their careers. They were *HOT* and their creative juices were flowing like lava from a volcano! Michael knew what he wanted from this album and according to several interviews with Quincy Jones and himself, took no time to put the album together. Michael yearned for this to be "the best" album ever, by any recording artist, and with his talents and intentions, accomplished exactly what he set his sights on. *Thriller*, released in November, 1982, was **THE BIGGEST SELLING ALBUM OF ALL TIME**, in the *history* of music, and still holds that illustrious title to date. The album broke records all around the world in countless countries and is epitomized in *history* for being recognized as the biggest selling album in numbers by *The Guinness Book of World Records*. When *Thriller* was released, I don't think anyone knew, not even Michael himself, what a major impact this album would have on the music industry and the pop culture of the 80's. It influenced the way we dressed, the way we danced, the course of music *history* itself—it was a complete revolution of a decade, all because of one man; *Michael Jackson*.

The brilliantly arranged music of *Thriller* fuses together

the sounds of Pop, Rock, Soul, and even Jazz, along with the musical contributions of several renowned musicians, into the most outstanding masterpiece of music ever produced. *Thriller* spawned an unparalleled 7 hit singles from one album—"Wanna Be Startin' Somethin'," "The Girl Is Mine," "Beat It," "Billie Jean," "Human Nature," "P.Y.T.," and the title cut itself, "Thriller."

    The first single release, "The Girl Is Mine," which was a duet with Paul McCartney, was not, in my opinion, the best choice for a first single release from an album that had so much more to offer. Truthfully, it was not a song that his fans wanted or expected from him and didn't fare as well as anticipated by Epic Records. They didn't even produce a video for this song as a promotion. I honestly don't think Michael's fans were ready for this sound just yet, as they were accustomed to his R & B music, and this song really was geared at a "White" audience. We didn't realize it then, but Michael's record company did that for a reason—they wanted him to "crossover" and appeal to a wider audience, thus gaining more success for Michael and grossing more profits for his record label. And who better than Paul McCartney, an ex-member of one of the biggest groups in music *history*, the Beatles, to team up with Michael for the debut single of his new album! It may have caught our attention, but not for long. The 6 other hit singles followed with such magnitude and set the stage for what was about to become "the greatest show on earth" for Michael.

    Thriller won an unprecedented 7 Grammy awards in 4 different musical categories—Pop, Rock, Soul, and R & B, an accomplishment worthy of the highest recognition. *Off The Wall* only received 1 Grammy award for Best R & B Vocal Performance—Male, for the song "Don't Stop 'Til You Get

Enough," because it did not have the same crossover flavor. Even though it was very successful in sales figures, it did not win for Album of the Year, which would have been more sublime for Michael. But because Michael is a Black recording artist and his music a blend of Pop, Rock, Jazz, Soul, and R & B, why should his color dictate the category of music it is classified as? Yes he is Black, and his music definitely is based on Soul, but with the other musical spices and flavors mixed in, how can you classify it in only one category? Impossible! It is a serious injustice and disrespect to label Michael Jackson's music in only one category, and I'm so pleased that *Thriller* was his ticket in. Finally, another door was opened that other Black artists could go through and follow in Michael's footsteps.

The worldwide crossover success of Michael Jackson sparked a slew of "wanna-bes," people wanting to be like, look like, dress like, sound like, and act like Mr. Jackson. Of course I, for the past ten years, was practicing my dancing and singing as I was emulating the Jacksons in my bedroom. Except for the occasional school or house party, I didn't bring my Jackson routine outside my house. It was something I did for myself because I enjoyed it, but I didn't go around trying to be just like Michael Jackson every day of my life. But with the "wanna-bes" sprouting up all over and the popularity of the *Thriller* album, the start of a new trend evolved; *Michael Jackson Look Alike Contests*. Oh yes, once one contest came out, then another, and so on until it seemed like every place was having a Michael Jackson Look Alike Contest!

My friends and family persuaded me to enter my first "look alike/dance alike" contest, which was sponsored by one of New York City's top R & B radio stations, 98.7 Kiss FM, and hosted by Yvonne Mobley, radio personality from Kiss FM. The event was held at Manhattan Center and featured about a dozen or so Michael Jackson look alike contestants. The other MJ's there were all dressed like Michael from either his *Off The Wall* album look or his *Thriller* look. Their performances were very good and the competition was tough, but deep down I somehow knew that I was going to win 1st place here. Even though these guys knew Michael Jackson and his style, they never studied him for years like I did. That alone gave me such an edge over them. When it came my turn to perform, and the first beat of "Billie Jean" hit, everyone, especially Yvonne Mobley, knew I had that show bagged! As I continued to electrify the audience with my routine, I realized then that this was going to be the start of something **BIG**!

This was my first Michael Jackson Look Alike contest that I won the Grand Prize of 1st place, and several more soon followed, all of which I won 1st place also. After the show, many people came to congratulate me on my performance and for winning first place. I spoke to a lot of people that evening, but one guy in particular, who was a well known D.J. in several clubs in New York, really praised my talents and wanted to become my manager. He was reputable throughout the New York area as a great D.J. and had many connections in all the clubs. He booked me in several of the hottest, most popular nightclubs of the time, including Leviticus, the Red Parrot, Chippendales, the Roxy, the Underground, Illusions, and the Funhouse. We were touring the whole New York metropolitan area, hitting all the hot spots, and meeting a lot of celebrities along the way, such as Ashford & Simpson, Patti Austin, Melba Moore, Kashif, New Edition, Harry Belafonte, plus numerous other influential people in the entertainment business.

My career as an impersonator had taken flight and I was performing every weekend, usually 2 - 4 shows per weekend, staying out until the wee hours of the morning. And women, women, women were flocking to me—women of every age and nationality were throwing themselves at me and I felt like a king with his "harem." I had groupies coming up to me after every show, offering all kinds of things. I finally got a taste of the whole "sex, drugs, and rock 'n roll" scene, only I never, ever would partake in any drugs or alcohol whatsoever! Believe me, I say it proudly, I keep my body clean and my mind clean! But the groupies were here, there, and everywhere, sneaking into my dressing room, hotel room, any room they could find me in! The best place to find me was backstage, and basically, this was where all the action took place. It got pretty wild at times; I could only imagine what some of the big rock stars really went through with the millions of fans and groupies coming on to them after every show! Women would do anything just to get with you—and believe me, they wanted to do it standing up, lying down, bending down, and bowing down!

    A good friend of mine that used to impersonate Prince would often get booked on the same shows as me and on many occasions, and would join me on stage during my performance. Imagine that; Prince and Michael Jackson on the same stage, *tearin' the mutha down*, where else could you see that! Only in America! Our specialty act generated twice the amount of women for the both of us, plenty to go around, and then some! One thing about my Prince impersonator friend, he's been with more women than it takes to talk about and would screw any woman, ready, willing, and able! But I'll never forget this one private function we both performed at, and the hostess of the party offered to pay us $5,000 together to spend the night with her. She was in her forties, quite wealthy, and obviously into Prince and Michael J. It was a very freaky scene, just like a

Rick James song, and we unanimously declined her offer. It wasn't because we didn't want the money—hey, $2,500 a piece isn't chump change! But truthfully, we didn't want to be used just for her sexual pleasure. Prince and Michael sharing the same stage is cool, but sharing the same woman is not. Yeah, we still had our morals, despite the temptation.

There was another incident where I met a popular female recording artist at a club in New York, who shall remain nameless, that was seriously involved with someone at the time, but seemed completely infatuated with me. She was hanging all over me that night, and after the promotional party we were attending, we ended up back at her hotel room for a midnight rendezvous. It was a lustful night of passion for the both of us, but needless to say, we never saw each other again. Life in the fast lane!

As I reminisce about my past encounters, one very funny story comes to mind, only it doesn't involve me, it involves another good friend of mine who used to impersonate PeeWee Herman. Back in 1987, we performed at a corporate function together and a woman, who was old enough to be his grandmother, approached him with a proposition, after flirting with him all night. She wanted to invite him back to her estate for a nightcap or two, and her limousine was waiting for her outside. He declined her invitation at first, but when she offered him a large sum of money that I cannot disclose, he pondered the thought for a moment and realized it wasn't so bad after all! As they were riding in luxury, en route to her "estate," she confessed her deepest, darkest secret to him—she always had an infatuation with PeeWee Herman and wanted him to fulfill one of her sexual fantasies as PeeWee. After a drink and some small talk, it was time for "PeeWee's Playhouse!" He willingly complied to her "desires" and performed doggie-style while wearing his red bow tie and white platform shoes! And at the climactic point of intercourse, he had to imitate that notorious, goofy laugh of PeeWee Herman's! So much for PeeWee's "big adventure!"

May 1983 marked another momentous event in music *history*—the television broadcast of the two hour special, "Motown 25: Yesterday, Today, Forever." The star-studded extravaganza celebrated the 25th anniversary of Motown Records and reunited several former Motown groups, including the Jackson Five. It was like the "Motor City Revue" of the 80's with such a multitude of stars performing under one roof. Only now they were all glamorized; they all looked like stars with their plastic surgeries and elaborate costumes, it was a beautiful thing. Long gone are the days of the "chitlin' circuit" for Motown's legendary artists.

This show featured some of Motown's most legendary performers, but I'm sure most would agree, the Jackson Five's reunion with brother Jermaine and the solo performance of Michael was the most memorable and most outstanding performance of the evening. Think about it—what else do you remember about that show? When those brothers hit that stage and recaptured the magic and excitement of their prime years as the Jackson Five, it was a rebirth of the Jackson-mania all over again! They just came back and conquered with their mighty performance!

While watching the telecast at home, I noticed one young boy in the audience who jumped way out of his seat, obviously overcome with joy and excitement from seeing the Jacksons "live." As I watched this little kid with the awe-struck expression on his face, it reminded me of myself as a child, studying the Jacksons' performance with such intensity and admiration, that even I jumped up after their performances, overcome by the spirit that moved me! Here I was again, watching the Jacksons perform and jumping out of my seat after their awesome performance! Seems like old times!

Then the Jacksons left the stage and brother Michael took over center stage and performed his famous hit, "Billie Jean." This song became Michael's "anthem" for the *Thriller* era and most widely recognized performance of his time. This was the launching pad for Michael's career which blasted off into orbit and skyrocketed into the next dimension! His moves were as graceful as a ballet dancers, and looked as though he was walking and gliding on air. Then he dazzled us with his world-famous dance step—the Moonwalk—which also became his trademark. No one can do the Moonwalk like Michael Jackson! Millions of people across the globe had tuned in to watch this Motown extravaganza, which was one of the highest rated music specials in television *history*!

The next day after Michael's electrifying performance, my entire neighborhood—friends, family, and neighbors—were spellbound by the magic of Michael's performance and the reunion of his brothers together again with brother Jermaine. It was the first time that all of the Jackson brothers shared the stage together since their last performance on "The Midnight Special" in 1979, which was hosted by the Jacksons themselves. Actually, the first time the Jacksons performed on television without brother Jermaine was in the summer of '75 on "The Mike Douglas Show," filmed in Las Vegas. Prior to that, Jermaine's last performance with his brothers on television was on "American Bandstand" in June 1975. And the first television appearance of "The Jacksons," no longer called the Jackson Five, was in September 1976 on the first episode of the new "Sonny & Cher" variety show. How's that for Jackson trivia?!

CHAPTER 13
The King Of Pop

Although the 80's spawned the birth of music videos and MTV, little did we know that Michael Jackson would change the *history* of music by revolutionizing the music style for the 80's—Pop Music. Pop music had originated in the late 70's, but it was Michael Jackson and *Thriller* that actually set the trend for Pop music of the decade. And look at the multitude of artists that soon followed behind Michael, like a caravan of Pop wanna-bes. "Pop stars." Michael Jackson had broken down barriers and walls for himself, as well as for other artists. He had crossed over with success in the music industry when there have been so many artists that have tried to do the same, but did not succeed like Michael. He has paved the way for countless artists, even up to this day, with his phenomenal success by being the 1st Black artist to have his video played on MTV. "One small step for man, one giant leap for mankind!" This gave Michael a broader, more culturally diversified group of fans of all ages, races, and musical tastes.

But if it wasn't for CBS Records threatening to pull all of their currently running videos featuring every one of their artists, off of MTV, if they didn't play Michael's videos, then perhaps MTV would never have shown Michael Jackson's or any other Black artists' videos. It took extreme and drastic measures by CBS Records to convince the head honchos at MTV that there was a very large audience out there that they were overlooking, and that was the Black audience. Just when Black people thought they were achieving equality after so many years of slavery, apartheid, segregation, and discrimination, here it is, life in the 80's, where there have been so many Black artists that have pioneered their way in the entertainment industry in order for Michael Jackson to be where he is, and there's still that much discrimination and segregation in the industry. Music is supposed to be the universal language that we all can understand and unite together in love, peace, and harmony. There have been numerous politicians, civil rights leaders, and religious leaders that have tried to unite the world with their teachings, words of wisdom, and laws, but they were only able to scratch the surface of what music has been doing for centuries. And after Michael Jackson broke through the barriers of MTV, another new music style was beginning to rise and challenge the network once again—*Rap music*!

    Rap music was a sound that many thought would come and go, like a fad, but the young Black generation were searching for a sound they could call all their own, and Rap music was their creation, their work of art. This form of music originated in the streets of the inner-city ghettos, where there was an entire "underworld" of talent waiting to be heard and discovered. Rap music is a unique sound consisting of hypnotic, constant beats and poetic words of pain, poverty, life, death, love, money, happiness; whatever emotions or realities exist in our lives. This music became a salvation to America's Black youth because it provided the opportunity for the Rap artists to achieve success from their creative art form as well as giving the Black children someone representative of their culture that they could idolize and look up to. My generation had the Jackson Five, who were the first Black idols, or rather heroes, that gave the Black children hope, encouragement, and the will to follow their dreams. But now we have a whole new generation of young Black artists for today's children to plug into.

Rap music has cultivated itself into the mass market, crossing over all boundaries, and had "White" America in an uproar, completely against it, even going so far as trying to ban it from all mediums. These conservative extremists were so afraid that their children would be exposed to something that could possibly integrate and unite their children with the Black teens. They certainly didn't want their children to learn about the oppression, the violence, the struggle, the destruction... the other side of life that they are afraid would be revealed to their children and the truth would come out. But statistics show, and it is a fact, that the record buying audience of Rap music and its artists, is predominantly young White teens. And Rap artists today can make millions, not thousands, of dollars off record sales alone. The impact of Rap music on its society has grown so large that the White conservatives cannot control this musical phenomenon. It is like osmosis.

Throughout Rap's *history*, there have been some rappers that have crossed over into mainstream, thereby opening more doors for other Rap artist to go through. Thanks to artists like Grand Master Flash, Run DMC, Ice T, Hammer, NWA, and Public Enemy, many different Rap styles evolved and are still being created, allowing for more crossover potential and popularity. We even had our first White rapper that crossed over and sold millions—remember Vanilla Ice? Homeboy jumped on the scene, cashed in at the right time and made millions, but his mass appeal didn't have longevity, so he was forced out of the Rap industry. Frankly, I think *The Teenage Mutant Ninja Turtles* movie killed it for him, but that's just my opinion.

While Rap music's influence increased beyond belief, everyone had to conform to the changes in contemporary music. New categories had to be added to the music award shows, radio station formats, music publications, music ratings and charts, retail music stores, and music television shows, like MTV, to properly define the music that was being created. MTV did not jump on the Rap bandwagon and help promote this flourishing music trend; instead it waited in the wings until Rap music took flight and then it seized the golden opportunity to grab hold of its tail and soar to higher plateaus, watching the $$'s roll in. Obviously Rap is here to stay, despite the disrespects, the criticisms, and the discriminations, it has survived, just like us Black folk, and still continues on stronger than ever.

CHAPTER 14

Human Nature

My career as a Michael Jackson impersonator had skyrocketed and I was out performing every weekend, nonstop. And I loved it. I have been blessed to have been given the opportunity to perform in front of tens of thousands of people, in countless venues across the country, and have made so many people *happy* with my performances. I am honored that I've been given the talent to impersonate the world's biggest, most successful entertainer in *history*... Michael Jackson, successfully. But what I am most thankful for are the people that not only complimented me on my uncanny resemblance and impersonation of Michael Jackson, but for my own God-given talent as a dancer and singer that has shined through every performance, and people have commended me for it. It feels so wonderful to have successfully convinced audiences that I was like the mirror image of Michael Jackson and to many youngsters, I was the real Michael Jackson. To impersonate someone of great talent and magnitude as Michael Jackson is not as easy as some may think. Just because someone can sing or dance, does not mean they can impersonate a multi-talented celebrity such as Michael Jackson. It's like the old clichés of stereotype thinking... just because you're Black doesn't mean you can play basketball. But to be able to emulate someone with such extraordinary talent, far beyond the limits of most, is a representation of my talent and ability as a performer. And I love to perform and make people *happy*, especially those very special children who are angels here on earth.

I fondly remember one particular little boy from Long Island, New York, that I will call Dre* (not his real name), whom I had the pleasure of performing for and making his dream come true. Dre was terminally ill with a rare bone disorder and wanted, more than anything in this world, to meet Michael Jackson. With the charitable work of the Make a Wish Foundation, I was chosen to fulfill his dream of meeting Michael Jackson. He had unfortunately missed perhaps the opportunity of a lifetime, meeting the King of Pop himself when the Make a Wish Foundation surprised him with 2 tickets to the Jacksons' 1984 Victory Tour concert at Madison Square Garden in New York City, and was unable to attend due to his illness. Dre's parents went to the concert for him, in the spirit of him, to see the show and get an autograph for him from Michael Jackson. And since Dre was not able to see Michael perform "live," his next wish was to have Michael Jackson come to his birthday party. So I did!

When I arrived at Dre's house, his entire street of neighbors were lined up and down the block, waiting outside to greet me. They clapped and cheered for me as my limousine drove through the crowd and pulled up in front of Dre's house. And by the way, the limo was provided by the Make a Wish Foundation because I refused any payment for this event, but they insisted on providing first class transportation for me, and the limousine was their choice. So, I'm feeling like one of the Beatles arriving in America for the first time, walking off the plane, in front of a crowd of screaming fans waiting for hours at the airport! Only the reality is I'm stepping out of a limo on a quiet street in the middle of suburbia with about 5% of the amount of fans, but the same amount of warmth and enthusiasm as I greet everyone with handshakes and hugs.

Simultaneously, the entire group of people separated right down the middle, like Moses' parting of the Red Sea, and there before me stood little Dre, with the look of admiration and love that only an idol or hero can bring to a child that adores them. He ran over to me and embraced me with a big hug that was filled with such warmth and sincerity that you couldn't help but love this child. During my visit with Dre, I performed all his favorite songs—"Beat It," "Thriller" and "Billie Jean"—and got the grand tour of his house to see his enormous Michael Jackson collection. After my tour, Dre's parents pulled me aside to explain to me why they had photos of Michael from the 1984 Victory Tour, but Dre wasn't in any of them because he could not go. Since Dre could not attend the most highly publicized, record-breaking concert ever, his father was determined to get an autograph and some pictures of Michael Jackson and his brothers, as momentos for his son. Dre was so ecstatic and full of joy when his parents went to the hospital to see him and gave him the photos and autographs of Michael Jackson, signed exclusively for him. Even though it was a dream come true for Dre to get an autograph from Michael Jackson and some candid photos of the Jacksons taken backstage, his parents knew Dre wanted to meet Michael Jackson in person more than anything in the world. I'm just so thankful that I was chosen by the wonderful people of the Make a Wish Foundation to fulfill this little boy's dream.

After spending the day with Dre and talking with him, I was amazed at the strength and bravery he possessed at such a young age in coping with his illness. He has an amazing spirit that just warms your heart, especially when he smiles. Just before I left, he pulled me over to him and gave me one last big hug and looked at me with tears of joy in his eyes and told me I made this the happiest day of his life. Tears came to my eyes as I walked away thinking there really are angels here on earth. Dre may not know it but he certainly was my hero that day, a day that I'll always cherish. I have not seen or spoken with Dre since that special day, but I know that God is with him, wherever he may be, and he is in my prayers.

Another angel that captured my heart with her spirit, wisdom, bravery, liveliness, and most of all, her sweetness, is a young "lady" whom I'll call "Angel." She is like a child sent by God with a purpose; she is like a real angel; she is chosen; she is sent here from heaven to enlighten the world about the horrible disease she has called AIDS. It's such a shame that an innocent child, like Angel, or any child in this world, should have to suffer from this horrific disease. You can't help but be enraptured by her spirit as she walks through life with a halo around her head. Even her mother realizes this gift from God that she has and the power this child possesses. It's unfortunate to say, but if it wasn't for someone as special as Angel and other notable innocent AIDS victims, such as Ryan White and Sharon Glaser, speaking openly and honestly to the world about their illness, people would not be as conscious and aware of the impact the AIDS virus has on destroying the human race. They have all upheld their dignity, their spirit, their faith, and love through the good, bad, and worse times of their illness that has claimed their lives and the lives of countless others, except for Angel.

People should be thankful for so many things, the little things, that are always taken for granted: the air in which we breathe, water which we thirst for, the sun that shines light upon us, the earth on which we walk upon, and our human existence itself. Even without these beautiful elements of nature, we could not exist. There are so many people in this world that are ignorant to the AIDS epidemic and are focusing on the materialistic things in life like greed, money, social status, racism, power, that become irrelevant when this deadly disease comes knocking upon their door. They would sacrifice everything if it would guarantee them a cure. But then and only then.

Each time I see this child, Angel, on any television program, I can feel her presence right there in the same room with me, and a warm spiritual feeling overcomes me. I just wish that I could reach out into the TV and give her a big hug, and assure her that there is a cure for this deadly disease and she would no longer have to suffer, physically. Maybe someday there will be a cure for this horrifying disease that has been plaguing the world ... but until then Angel, I love you for you are an inspiration to humanity. God Bless You.

TOUCHED BY THE JACKSONS

CHAPTER 15
Working Day And Night

Undoubtedly, 1984 was the most hectic year of my career as a Michael Jackson lookalike, and I was performing up to 10 shows per week. Up until this point I was making my own Jackson costumes because I couldn't afford to pay a costume designer for their work, and had to do it all myself; sewing sequins onto my shirts, socks, and white gloves, to complete the MJ ensemble. But it was getting so chaotic that I couldn't keep up with all the maintenance of cleaning and repairing the costumes and had no choice but to call upon a designer to create some more durable, yet flashy, stage-like, authentic Jackson-style costumes, and keep up with the maintenance for me. But believe me, it was worth the investment. I had professional costumes that no one else had, and it showed!

I also needed the costumes because I was traveling and getting booked all over the world in places like Los Angeles, Florida, West Virginia, Calgary, Canada, Las Vegas, Barbados, South Carolina, etc., and didn't have the time anymore. Hey, I was touring! And it was a dream come true! One of the largest venues and events I ever played was in Barbados. The week long event was being publicized all over the island, on radio, television, in the newspapers, even on posters hanging on poles and trees everywhere you went! It was awesome to see so much promotion of myself in a foreign country that I really did feel like Michael Jackson! I did several on air radio interviews to promote myself and the week long event at the prestigious resort I was performing at, along with a very well known Caribbean band from New York that had been traveling to Barbados faithfully for many years. The natives were very gracious and hospitable and went out on a limb for us at any expense. Even the receptionist at the hotel offered me a guided tour around town and a night out at the movies, her treat. It's not that often a woman takes a man out, so I decided to jump on her generous offer and hit the town! We went to dinner first and then to the local drive-in movie—my first time ever—and saw the movie *Breakin'*. I couldn't stay out too late because I had a show that night and needed time to prepare, so she drove me back to the hotel. I thanked her for the fun and exciting evening, but when I went to get out of her car, she wrapped herself around me like an octopus and wouldn't let go! I had to pry myself out of her grip and make a mad dash for the hotel room before it was too late.

Back in my room safely, I told my manager about my little outing, spilling out all the details about the "octopus woman" and our evening together. He was very concerned and explained to me that I really have to be more careful about my own security and safety. I took a big risk going out with a strange woman in a foreign country that I knew nothing about except for her first name and where she worked and didn't tell anyone where I was going. Also being out in public without any security guards could open myself up to some possible unwanted jealousies and unfriendly people wanting to hurt me or something. In other words, I messed up. Had I known then what I know now, I wouldn't have been so trusting of people and would have taken more precautions. I can speak now from experience because in my life, since I'm so generous and caring and open my heart to people, I have let some of the wrong people get too close to me, at my own expense. For one reason or another they've tried to take advantage of my kindness and use me, knowing my heart bleeds easily and I will do all that I can to help someone. I've learned over the years as I matured and became wiser that I can't let my guards down with people and trust them until I know them for sure. Especially groupies.

There was one female fan that I have to call a "groupie" that came to every one of my performances at this one particular club in New York. She would always take pictures of me and bring copies of the photos to my next gig as a ticket to get backstage. When she did get in to see me, she would always ask me to go out with her and flirt with me like crazy, but I just didn't dig her. She was too pushy and aggressive for my liking, so I kept turning her down. I must have said "no" one too many times and offended her because she got very loud with me and stormed out of the club, like I was supposed to follow her or something. Frankly, I was a bit relieved because I really don't like to keep saying no to people and disappointing them, but sometimes you have to.

After a while, one of her girlfriends approached me and told me not to go out the back door of the club when I leave because there were a few thugs waiting to jump me; the kind of guys you don't want to meet in a dark alley. So when I left, I went out the front door, of course, and caught a taxi cab home. Somebody was watching over me that night because I had no problems catching a cab for a change, (being a Black man, it is often a problem), and got home quickly and safely! And thank God, never saw that girl again. But think about it—if I'm going through this with some crazed fans, just imagine all the crazy shit the Jacksons had to go through with the millions of fans they have all over the world! That is f***ing scary! I even had another horrifying experience that stemmed from nothing but pure jealousy.

I was doing an outdoor promotional event and after the show, this man approached me saying that he recognized me from a previous engagement. He caught an attitude with me immediately, trying to huff and puff his weight around, I guess trying to intimidate me. For whatever reason, whether his girlfriend liked me or was obsessed with Michael Jackson, or he was just simply jealous, he purposely tried to instigate a fight with me. When he saw that I wasn't giving in to his little ego trip game, he pulled out a box cutter razor and went straight for my face. He only barely nicked my face on my chin. My people saw what was happening and instantly jumped to my rescue and beat the shit out of him. Then they chased the guy away, like he was a stray dog. After we kicked his ass, and two broken knuckles later, the only thing we ever found out about this guy was his name was Elvis. Imagine that, a Black guy named Elvis!

But soon I was off to Las Vegas where I encountered yet another Elvis, only he was an impersonator, like me, in the world renowned Legends show. We met after one of his performances and the thing that really impressed me about him was that he was the only Elvis impersonator licensed by the Graceland Estate to perform as Elvis at that time. I've never heard of someone actually being licensed to do this and it meant that he was the best at what he did and I thought that was such an accomplishment.

I went to Las Vegas to perform at the Model of the Year Competition, Grand Finals, at the Sahara Hotel in the summer of 1984. It was a week long competition for some of the most beautiful women I have ever seen. It was very exciting. I had the opportunity to appear on the same stage that many legendary stars have performed on over the years, just like the Apollo Theater. We stayed in the same hotel that the legendary comedian, Redd Foxx, was staying in and was fortunate to have met him off stage. He was gracious enough to give us comp tickets to see his show one night and I was more than thrilled to see him do his stand-up routine "live." I've heard so much about Redd Foxx's shows being raunchy, explicit, even vulgar, but I enjoyed it—it wasn't as dirty as I thought. I was ecstatic to have seen one of the world's greatest Black stand-up comedians perform live, who was a legend in his own time.

During my stay in Las Vegas, I got booked at one of the hottest nightclubs by my manager. He was always trying to hustle up some shows for us, to get me out there in front of the public. So while we were standing in the lounge area of the club waiting for my time to go on, a group of men walked in and noticed us in the lounge. They kept staring at me and the first thing I thought was they had never seen a Michael Jackson look alike before, or even worse, had never seen a Black man before. They finally came over to approach me and asked me why I was wearing this jacket. I was wearing a Marine Corps jacket to duplicate one of Michael Jackson's military jackets, only I obviously had an authentic one. I explained to them that it was a part of my persona, impersonating Michael Jackson, and they accepted my answer and walked away. After having a drink or two, they decided to come back and said they were very offended by me wearing this jacket because it is genuine and represents a serviceman of the Marines. They also said this particular jacket is worn for funerals of another Marine cadet and when they appear with the President of the United States. One guy come right up to me and said, "If I was you, I'd take that jacket off." I apologized if I offended him and his buddies because I wasn't trying to disrespect anybody, it was just a part of my costume. The club's manager finally came over and pulled me aside for a second, away from the drunken Marines. He kindly and respectably asked me to remove my jacket because these guys were being assholes and he didn't want a big barroom brawl over a jacket in his club. Since I was ready to start my show, I finally took off "the jacket" and gave it to my manager.

During my performance, everyone was standing up, dancing and screaming for me, including the gentlemen from the Marines. It's amazing how music can make us all come together in happiness and make us forget the negative things in this world, especially something as minor as a jacket.

It was time for the Grand Finals competition and I was the featured entertainment for the event. Of course the ladies were enough entertainment for me, but I was a part of the show, too. I dazzled the audience with my performance of Michael Jackson's "Don't Stop 'Til You Get Enough," and "Billie Jean" and their response was phenomenal! They just went nuts over me and I got 2 standing ovations! It was incredible! I came back out to take another bow and got another standing ovation from the audience! I couldn't believe it! I wondered if they thought I was the real Michael Jackson or something because this was the most receptive audience I had ever had. I was flying high together with my manager because I felt like Michael Jackson himself the way the crowd had received me. It was one of the most memorable events in my career that I'll always remember.

CHAPTER 16
I Found That Girl

I was so involved with my career at this time that Malka and I came to a decision to end our relationship together, but I still maintained a close relationship with my two sons no matter what. To this day, we have a good, healthy, mutual parent relationship because we parted on good terms. Malka never wanted to stand in the way of my career and dreams and for that, I respect her. She was just not ready to follow my dreams with me.

One special day, at one of my shows, which was a promotional party for CBS Records at New York's famous Chippendales nightclub, I met the woman of my life, Kristine, my friend who would become my wife and mother of my two youngest sons. At the CBS party, which was comprised mostly of music industry executives, they were showing a lot of Michael Jackson and the Jacksons videos on their giant screens, like it was a Jackson promotional party only!

While I was performing, I couldn't help but notice a young lady staring at me from the dance floor, looking up at me on the stage. Everyone was dancing and having a good time, except for her. She was studying my every move like a hawk to see if I had mastered the Gloved One's moves. After my show, a lot of females surrounded me to get my autograph, buy me a drink, give me their phone numbers, etc., except for her. She approached my manager first, who escorted her into my dressing room to meet me. We went to sit in the lounge area overlooking the dance floor and had a long conversation about Michael Jackson and my career as an impersonator. She told me she got an invitation to the CBS party from one of her coworkers and brought some of her college friends with her. She told me that she really was impressed with my performance and wanted to give me a few make-up tips to enhance my look, if given the opportunity to do so.

I gave Kristine an 8 x 10 glossy photo of myself and we exchanged phone numbers. I actually received several phone numbers that evening from young women and some older women, too, that liked me. She tried to call my house 2 to 3 times a day for a few days, but I would never speak to her. I tried to avoid her and kept brushing her off because I really wasn't interested; she wasn't my type. Finally, after about a week or so, I took her phone call and ended up making a date with her. The rest, as they say, is *history*.

CHAPTER 17
Victory

The Jacksons had embarked upon what was titled the "Concert of the Century"—the Jacksons' 1984 Victory Tour. It was a celebrated reunion of every last member, all six of the Jackson brothers: Jackie, Marlon, Michael, Tito, Jermaine, and Randy. The Jacksons' Victory Tour was so lavish and extravagant, only superlatives can be used to describe it. It was a show that should not have been missed by anyone; it was *history* in the making. To date there has never been a concert tour of such magnitude. The media attention alone it received made it by far the most highly publicized concert event in music *history*. The elaborate production costs have exceeded over $15 million dollars and the operational costs per week were over $1 million dollars. The Jacksons' Victory Tour grossed an estimated $75 million dollars plus, as it sold out stadiums from New York to Los Angeles. The Jacksons worked endlessly preparing for the tour and collaborated on the stage design, stage productions, and special effects. The impressive 5 story high stage was surrounded by a sea of thousands of multicolored lights, whirling lasers of red, green, and yellow, and powerful explosives.

I have been so very fortunate to have been able to see the Jacksons at their three New Jersey shows at Giants Stadium in East Rutherford, NJ on July 29th, 30th, and 31st, 1984, and their two New York appearances at Madison Square Garden in New York City, August 4th and 5th, 1984. Each individual show was outstanding, but I enjoyed their performances at Madison Square Garden in New York City much more because even though I obtained "All Access" passes to both the NY and NJ shows, Madison Square Garden is a smaller venue and I was able to stand right next to the stage, within an arms length of the Jacksons! When Kristine and I arrived at MSG with our All Access passes in hand, we were escorted to a special elevator, which took us to the ground level of the Jacksons' magnificent stage. It was so amazing to see the Jacksons so close, you could hear their footsteps on the stage as they danced, hear them talking and breathing between verses, and see every drop of sweat that came off their bodies. There was so much brotherly love generating up on that stage between the brothers that despite all the bad press that was written about them not getting along, it was clear to see in their eyes that there was genuine love for one another. The most touching moment I witnessed was during Michael's performance of "Billie Jean." Just before he went into his astonishing "Moonwalk" across the stage, brother Jermaine looked at Michael with such joy and sheer pride of his younger brother that it brought tears to my eyes to see this display of affection.

    For those of you that missed the "Concert of the Century," it all began in darkness. The entire arena went black as the sounds of slave-driving music amplified through the air. A chain gang of futuristic Muppet-like creatures, which stood about 10 feet tall, and were called Kreetons, entered the stage, one by one, marching to the beat of the accompanying music. There in the middle of the stage was a block of stone with a magical sword that possessed powers, stuck in the stone's core, like a Medieval fairy tale of sorts. A deep voice of hope echoed the words:

VICTORY

"Long, long ago, the Kreeton people walked the earth. They held people captive for slaves and bondage, bringing evil and ruin to what was good. These are the Kreeton people. Whoever would pull the sword from the stone would be king for years and years. It was prophesied that a mighty one would come and pull the sword from the stone and destroy the Kreeton people. This one would be called great, most holy and powerful. His kingdom shall be a kingdom that will never be brought to ruin. It will last from time indefinite 'til time indefinite. But who would pull the sword from the stone?"

As the mighty Randy Jackson, clad in a majestic suit of armor that covered his face, pulled the sword from the stone, the crowd cheered as the royal horns played the sounds of *victory*. The Kreetons' leader ordered his people, "Destroy him!" as the Kreetons surrounded Randy. Randy fought courageously for his kingdom as he beheld his mighty sword. With the first strike of the laser-type sword, Randy defeated the Kreetons. He then shouted out: "Arise all the world and behold the kingdom!" The sounds of thunder rolled as the storm of laser lightning bolts and clouds of smoke clashed as the sky opened up to reveal the power and glory of the Jacksons. There they stood, high up on a rising platform, as if they were some untouchable, spiritual beings. They slowly began to descend from the heavens down to the earth, and with each footstep, the earth shook, as the Jacksons made their way towards center stage. In unison, they removed their dark shades to reveal their identities—Tito, Marlon, Michael, Randy, and Jermaine. The crowd went into a roaring frenzy as the mighty Jacksons stood before them, bigger than life. When the crowd could no longer take the *torture* as they were in a *state of shock*, Michael signaled to the band that they were ready to **kick ass!!**

As soon as the first note of "Wanna Be Startin'

Somethin'" was played, the Jacksons exploded on the stage as the crowd went into a frenzy! The Jacksons gave a dynamic performance of their most famous hits from Michael's *Off The Wall* and *Thriller* albums, and the Jacksons' *Triumph* album. Brother Jermaine even took over center stage as he performed his hits, "Let's Get Serious," "Dynamite," and "Tell Me I'm Not Dreaming (Too Good To Be True)." Jermaine had total control of the crowd as they went wild with his medley of hits, singing every word along with him. He had the audience spellbound as they chanted "Dynamite!" back and forth with him during his performance of the song. He was then joined on-stage by brother Michael for their duet hit song, "Tell Me I'm Not Dreaming (Too Good To Be True)," which was the jam! I thought I was dreaming because it was *too good to be true* to have both Michael and Jermaine together again on stage singing a duet! The energy level never ceased throughout the entire show, all the way to their closing song, "Lovely One," which had everybody out of their seats, up on their feet, dancing!

After a long, thunderous applause by the audience, the Jacksons returned to the stage for their encore. They reappeared all freshened up in a new set of flashy costumes. The African beats started along with the ad-libs and vocal sounds of the Jacksons, as they broke into Michael's hit song, "Working Day and Night," from his megahit album, *Off The Wall*. The Jacksons mystified the audience with their synchronized dance steps to the high energy music, which they breakdown to just a rhythm of drum beats, a la Indian style, as they do their version of an Indian ceremonial dance! Randy then dons a silver sadistic looking mask and begins chasing Michael around the stage until he traps him at center stage. The beats ceased and the music changed to a haunting, horror movie theme, which was a bit unsettling. From up above, two giant mechanical one-eyed spiders came to life, as Randy summoned them towards Michael. These huge eerie monsters, covered in glowing white lights, descended down towards Michael, as he dramatically fell to the stage, crippled with fright! He repeatedly screamed 'No! No! No!" as one of the mechanical monsters closed in on its prey—Michael—and went for the kill! Michael collapsed from the spider's "venom" as the spider rose to its *victory*. Randy then took his silver cape off and laid it over Michael's body, covering him completely. The magic began as Michael's body started to rise as Randy created an illusion of levitation, while Michael floated higher and higher above the stage. Everyone watched with anticipation as Michael's covered body was magically suspended over center stage. Randy then grabbed the cape like a magician performing a grand illusion, and pulled it away as flashpots exploded to reveal.... nothing! Michael had completely vanished! At the right side of the stage, large pyrotechnical explosions go off as Michael reappeared in his famous red leather zippered jacket from his video "Beat It," along with brother Marlon. The guitar intro to "Beat It" led the crowd into a frenzied delight as they danced and sang to this rock favorite. After "Beat It," the stage went black for a few moments and a single spotlight hit Michael, as the opening beats of his multi-million selling hit, "Billie Jean" echoed throughout the arena. Michael was dressed in his black sequined jacket, black fedora hat, and rhinestone-studded white glove, still with his colorful "Beat It" shirt on under the jacket. Michael was smooth as he floated through every dance movement, and the crowd grew louder and louder with every step! This was the ultimate highlight of the entire concert for me and the anticipation level of the crowd was so high it was ready to burst! The band broke the music down to just the drum beats and Michael; it was his time to shine. He flowed like water with his graceful moves and then went into his world famous "Moonwalk," which left the crowd spellbound in awe! It was truly the climax of the show!

After "Billie Jean," the stage started to transform; hydraulic lifts raised the drummer Jonathan Moffet to a higher plateau, as the lights rotated and revolved side to side behind the Jacksons, with space age sound effects shooting through the air. The mighty Jacksons broke into their final encore song, their number 1 hit from the 1978 *Destiny* album, "Shake Your Body (Down to the Ground)." Just like their 1981 Triumph Tour, this was the song that took the house down! At the Sunday night show, there was a stage extension that came out from beneath the main stage, that provided a second lower level for the Jacksons to come down and get closer to the audience. Since this particular concert was indoors, the Jacksons could not put on the fireworks display that they had at their outdoor stadium shows; instead, they had pyrotechnics and a beautiful laser light show of many colors. As the Jackson made their final exit off the stage and said good night, all I could think of was that it felt like a dream to me. Never have I been so close, within 10 feet of the Jacksons performing "live!" It was about equal the excitement as meeting them in person, as I did when they were in New York City, making their preparations for the Victory Tour.

A good friend of mine who worked for 98.7 KISS FM Radio in New York, the one who provided me with the "All Access" passes to the Victory Tour shows at Giants Stadium and Madison Square Garden, was able to pull some strings for me, knowing how much I wanted to meet the Jacksons. He took me to their sound check rehearsal at Madison Square Garden where I was able to watch them behind the scenes doing what they do best. I was introduced to Michael, Marlon, Tito, and Randy Jackson, four of the six brothers that were my idols that I looked up to for so many years. Tito was very nice, considerate and patient, never trying to rush you. Marlon was so outgoing, friendly and full of spirit. Randy was rather shy and on the quiet side, and Michael was not as shy or weird as the public perceives him. He was very friendly and cordial, but yet a little bit timid. Even though our meeting was short, it was the most exciting 10 minutes of my life and I feel very fortunate and blessed to have been able to meet the Jacksons personally and see them perform live.

PHOTOGRAPHS

The Jackson Five posing at home, 1972. *

TOUCHED BY THE JACKSONS

The Jackson Five at a Motown recording session, 1971. *

Michael Jackson *with a child's heart.* *

PHOTOGRAPHS

Michael Jackson enjoying time off from his busy schedule, 1972. *

TOUCHED BY THE JACKSONS

Tito (top) and Jackie (below) Jackson on the set of their 1973 television special, "The Jackson Five." **

PHOTOGRAPHS

Jermaine (top) and Marlon (below) Jackson having fun during the taping of the Jackson Five's second television special, 1973.**

TOUCHED BY THE JACKSONS

Michael Jackson plays a *"teenage symphony"* during a break from shooting a television commercial, 1972. **

The Jackson Five enjoy a well-balanced breakfast...juice, toast, milk, and ABC's and 123's, during the taping of a Post Alpha-Bits cereal commercial, 1972. **

PHOTOGRAPHS

Michael Jackson has always been an admirer of hats. Photo taken at Weldon A. McDougal III's home, 1976. *

Phoenix tips his hat to the King of Pop! Photo taken at Weldon A. McDougal III's home 20 years later, 1996. *

TOUCHED BY THE JACKSONS

Michael Jackson backstage at a concert in Philadelphia, 1976. *

Michael Jackson poses for a photo after a recording session, 1976. *

Randy Jackson relaxing during a break from his hectic schedule, 1976. *

PHOTOGRAPHS

Michael Jackson performing "Don't Stop 'Til You Get Enough" during the 1981 Triumph Tour at Madison Square Garden, New York City. **

Michael Jackson in his hotel suite, at the Helmsley Palace in New York, 1983. **

Michael Jackson performing live during the Jacksons' 1981 Triumph Tour at Madison Square Garden, New York City. **

TOUCHED BY THE JACKSONS

Michael Jackson performing "Off The Wall" at the Jacksons' 1984 Victory Tour at Giants Stadium, East Rutherford, New Jersey. **

"Tell Me I'm Not Dreamin' " ... Jermaine on stage with his brothers again! This is *"too good to be true!"* **

Jermaine Jackson takes center stage and *"gets serious"* with brothers Randy and Marlon at the 1984 Victory Tour. **

PHOTOGRAPHS

Just a small portion of Phoenix's massive Jackson collection! **

TOUCHED BY THE JACKSONS

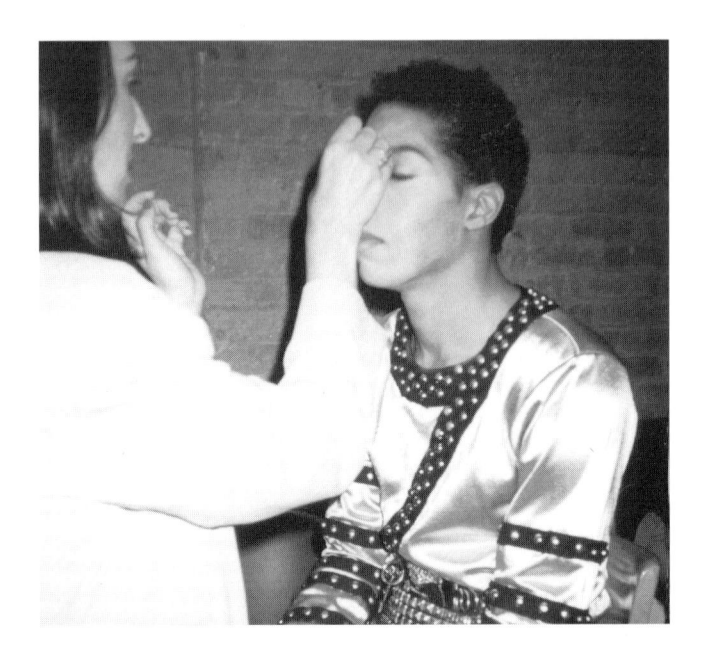

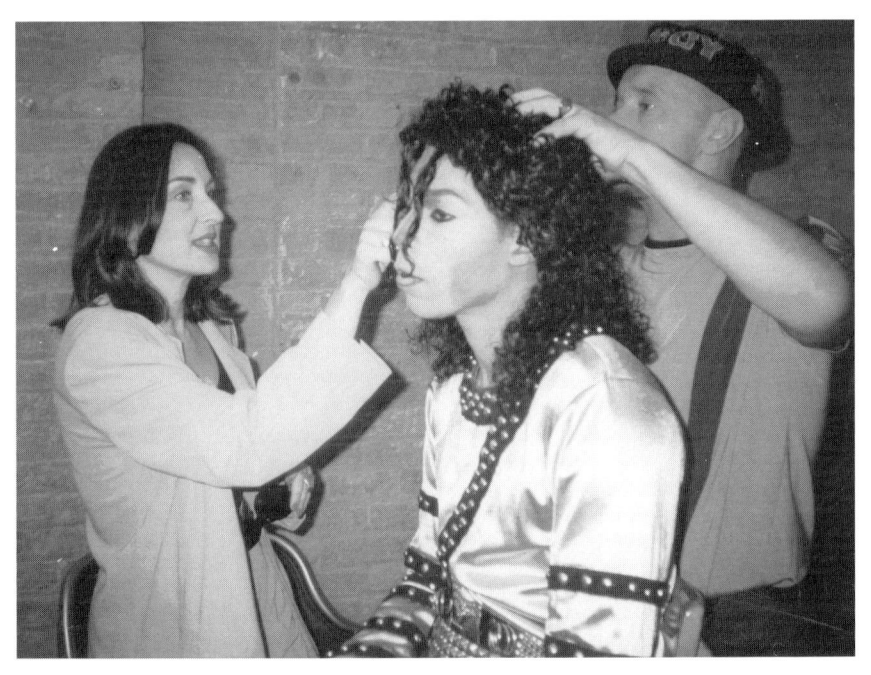

Phoenix "before and after" on the set of New York's "FOX 5 News," Michael Jackson Makeover, May 20, 1991." **

PHOTOGRAPHS

Producer Mark Bozack lends Phoenix a helping hand during the taping of the Michael Jackson Makeover, 1991. **

TOUCHED BY THE JACKSONS

Who's Bad? Phoenix!! (1991) **

PHOTOGRAPHS

"The mirrors of my mind." **

TOUCHED BY THE JACKSONS

The creative team of experts, Max Pinnell, Lydia Snyder, and Tony Melillo, with Phoenix as the transformed "Michael Jackson." **

The entire behind-the-scenes crew that made it all possible for Phoenix. **

PHOTOGRAPHS

Phoenix with Jermaine Jackson at the ABC Studios in New York City, Election Day, November 3, 1992. **

Phoenix and the man himself, Frank DiLeo, at the Kwanzaa Fest in the Jacob Javitz Center, New York City, December 16, 1995. **

TOUCHED BY THE JACKSONS

Taj Jackson feels the music as he performs 3T's #1 hit, "Anything" at the Kwanzaa Fest in New York City, December 16, 1995. **

Taryll Jackson blushes as the female fans scream his name at the Kwanzaa Fest. **

PHOTOGRAPHS

T.J. Jackson takes his performance seriously.**

3T spread their brotherly love at the Kwanzaa Fest in New York City, 1995. **

TOUCHED BY THE JACKSONS

Behind every great man there is a beautiful woman. Phoenix with his wife, Kristine. **

Phoenix and wife, Kristine, with their good friend, Smokey Robinson, backstage in Atlantic City, New Jersey, at the Trump Plaza Hotel & Casino, August 18, 1995. **

PHOTOGRAPHS

Phoenix with friends Smokey Robinson and Smokey's Tour Manager and Chief of Security, Earl Bryant, in Lake Tahoe, Nevada, at Caesar's Hotel & Casino, August 2, 1997. **

Phoenix with friend, Tony Lewis, Smokey Robinson's drummer, backstage after a performance in Atlantic City, New Jersey at the Trump Taj Mahal Hotel & Casino, June 22, 1996. **

TOUCHED BY THE JACKSONS

Joan Lunden with Phoenix as Michael Jackson at Tappan Hills in Tarrytown, New York on March 9, 1996. **

PHOTOGRAPHS

Looking through the windows... **

TOUCHED BY THE JACKSONS

Phoenix backstage after his opening performance for the then up-and-coming group, New Edition, in Queens, New York, February 18, 1984. **

CHAPTER 18
We Can Change The World

In the early part of 1985, Michael Jackson embarked upon a project that was one of his most divine works, simply for its cause alone. Michael, along with the collaborative efforts of long-time friend, Lionel Richie, composed a special song for famine relief in Africa, entitled "We Are The World," hoping to stop the starvation and desperation that had plagued the Motherland. Producer, Quincy Jones brought the musical masterpiece to life, with the help of over 40 recording artists, including the Jacksons, lending their vocals to the project, and "USA For Africa" was born. Bob Geldof, famed lead singer of the Boomtown Rats, initiated the movement with his own project in Britain called "Band Aid," a group of British/European artists singing together for a common purpose—famine relief in Africa.

The effort ignited a worldwide awareness of the heart-wrenching realization that millions of people were dying of starvation and individual groups and charities began answering the call for desperation. It was a beautiful, honorable, sincere, humanitarian endeavor by Bob Geldof, who alone first spoke out to the world for these helpless people who did not ask of him; he graciously became their voice crying out to the world. But because of him, the world heard their cries, and answered them. Relief projects all over the world, including USA For Africa, came to the aid of a nation that was on the verge of extinction.

"We Are The World" became the anthem and foundation for USA For Africa and its projects, with the help of its creators; Michael Jackson, Lionel Richie, and Quincy Jones. They, too, should be honored for their talents, as they are the ones who sparked the movement worldwide with their song that echoed throughout the world. USA For Africa was a major force in the efforts to aid famine relief, attracting the attention of the world with its celebrity representatives. But without them, the world would not have recognized the cause so urgently and the relief funds would have been minimal. I remember hearing "We Are The World" practically everywhere I turned—in school, at church, at home, blaring from car stereos, on television, etc., and it made me so *happy* to think that maybe we were saving one more life every time the song was played. And the more they played the song, the more positive I felt, knowing that it really was making a difference. The song itself certainly made its impact on the world as it became the first ever multi-Platinum single in music *history* and making its mark in the *History* books.

But how sad it is to think of all the people that suffered with such desperately hopeless conditions for so long that it took the voices of celebrity recording artists to open our ears and our hearts to the sounds of them dying. *"Faces... did you see their faces? Did they touch you? Have you felt such pain? To have nothing... to dream something... then lose hoping. Is not life but lame."* My ears and my heart bled from the sounds of my brothers and sisters crying out for food and water.... FOOD AND WATER!! Two basic necessities of life that we all take for granted every day. Just listen to the selfishness... " I only eat Beluga caviar." "I'm too tired to cook, let's get some pizza!'" "I can only drink bottled water—my tap water tastes funny." 'I don't like meatloaf; can I eat at Jimmy's house?" "Don't forget to pick up milk at the store!" We are all guilty of this behavior in some sort of way because we are spoiled with endless choices and variety in our modern society. But what if our choices were "Should I drink from this river because it might be contaminated?" "Which child gets to eat the only piece of yam I have left?" "How many days do we have to travel to find some food?" "Will there be food when we get there?" Or "will I survive the trip because I am too weak?" These are life or death choices; choices we pray we never have to make... choices we pray no one will ever have to make anymore. *"Always... please be not always. 'Cause if always... bow our heads in blame. 'Cause time has made promises... death promises."*

CHAPTER 19

Frontiers

Michael Jackson starred in his first short film ever for Disney, which was a 17 minute long musical journey through space, featuring Michael Jackson as "Captain Eo." The *Captain Eo* movie was a featured attraction at the Disney World theme park, complete with dazzling 3-D effects and digitalized surround sound which gave you the realistic feeling of being a part of the movie itself.

Captain Eo, along with his space companions, Hooter, Fuzzball, Major Domo and Minor Domo, and the Geeks—Idie & Odie, are summoned by his superior, Commander Bog, to bring a special gift to the Supreme Leader, better known as the Witch Queen of the Dark Planet. The Witch Queen is an evil, wicked, ugly, black widow-looking leader of a planet filled with darkness, despair, and gloom. The special gift he is to bring to the Witch Queen is the gift of "love." When Captain Eo arrives on the Dark Planet, he presents himself to the Supreme Leader, the Witch Queen, to state his purpose of business on the planet. Captain Eo tells the Queen he has a gift for her because she is very beautiful within, but without a key to unlock it, which is his gift to her. Captain Eo and his comrades then work their musical magic on her with their song "We Are Here To Change The World." Once she is entranced by the music, Captain Eo then zaps her with the magic of "love." The Queen of Darkness slowly transforms into a beautiful, radiant woman and Captain Eo restores all the beautiful colors of her planet once again, so it now looks like paradise. The mini movie ends with another song by Michael, a.k.a. Captain Eo, "Another Part of Me," as Michael hugs the Queen good-bye and bids everyone a fine farewell. Mission accomplished!

In reality, this is something that Michael Jackson truly does with his music; he brings joy, happiness, and love to all, which in turn, brings out the best in people. Their inner beauty shines right through. And just like his song, "We Are Here To Change The World," we should all try to change ourselves to make this world a better place because in order to change yourself, you have to start with the *man in the mirror*, and this is *just another part of* Michael Jackson. For these are *precious moments*, for brother Jermaine, that is.

During the same year, brother Jermaine Jackson embarked upon his 1986 Precious Moments Tour, with the release of his album of the same name. This was one tour that I was completely unable to attend, due to my busy schedule, even when Jermaine played at New York City's world-famous Apollo Theater. I was very sad I couldn't attend any of his shows because this was the year that Jermaine's career really took a turn in the right direction for him. The biggest hits of the year were, "I Think It's Love," "Do You Remember Me?," "Words Into Action," and "I Hear a Heartbreak." Jermaine was even sporting a new longhaired look for the year, too. Even though I prefer to see all of the Jackson brother perform together, Jermaine, the first brother to leave the group to pursue his solo career in 1976, had clearly proven himself as an established solo artist. His soulful music, mostly romantic love ballads, are classic, timeless hits that will always be around. And Jermaine's vocal style will only get better with age, like a fine wine. Also, what I really admire about Jermaine as a solo artist is that even though he is a "Jackson," he lets his own individual musical style come through, instead of trying to do everything Jackson-style. Hey, *his name is Jermaine!*

CHAPTER 20
Gone Too Soon

One hot evening in July, I came home and my fiancee, Kristine, told me she had heard Michael Jackson's new single release, "I Just Can't Stop Loving You," on the radio that day. Frankly, I was kind of shocked to hear that this song was chosen to be his 1st single release off his new album. It was a soft, romantic duet that only had limited appeal to Michael's listening audience. The public is used to Michael coming out with something more funky... more up tempo, than "I Just Can't Stop Loving You." But technically, when Michael Jackson released *Thriller*, the first single release from the album was "The Girl Is Mine," a duet with legendary ex-Beatle, Paul McCartney. CBS executives obviously wanted to market this album to a "White" audience, but Michael's Black fans did not welcome it, as they anticipated. Michael, the eternally famous superstar in the industry for over a decade, has a tremendous worldwide audience of his own. But what were the head honchos over at CBS thinking when they did this!? Didn't they see that this man's skin is Black? Didn't they know what kind of music he created and who his audience was? What everyone wanted, what they expected, was the world-famous Jackson sound and "The Girl Is Mine" just could not deliver. And neither could "I Just Can't Stop Loving You."

"Bad," which was to become Michael's biggest selling hit was "the one" that his audience was waiting for from this album. Especially since MTV and CBS decided to premiere this video, the single became even more popular and Michael found his pot o' gold at the end of his rainbow! But "I Just Can't Stop Loving You" was not the best choice for the 1st single release from his new, soon-to-be-released album, *Bad*. *Bad*, released August 31, 1987, offered a surprisingly new Pop sound all its own, and Michael was the one to deliver it. Along with producer Quincy Jones, Michael created a digitalized and computerized sound, using the latest in state-of-the-art recording equipment, which made the sound phenomenal! The multi-levels of sounds that were produced from this digitalized equipment were recorded at such a very high volume, you could very well shatter your speakers if your volume was up too high.

    The music video, *Bad*, the first video release from the album of the same name, premiered on August 31, 1987, same day as the *Bad* album. The touching story centered on a young man and the friends he grew up with in the "ghetto." And just like all the stories you've heard about a group of young Black men from the inner-city ghettos, and out of all of these friends, a few, maybe even only one, will make something of himself and achieve his goals. The rest either end up in jail or dead, usually as a result of violence involving guns and drugs. The statistics are staggering; 80% of Black men 21 and under will die as a result of drugs or gang violence. But if we don't try to stop these statistics of genocidal violence from escalating, the numbers will soon be 99%! What the young Black brothers have to realize is that this is genocide, and it is true that this is what "The Man" wants, to see you go no where but down under. We as a people have to be smarter than that and not fall victim to the game plan.

    In the *Bad* music video, it's a story of 4 young Black men from Harlem, who grew up together, but one of them follows his road to success while the others are to become statistics. The main character, Daryl, portrayed by Michael Jackson, grew up with his buddies in the streets, stealing, cheating, hustling, but happened to be smart enough to stay in school and went on to college. During one winter break, he came home and realized, after being exposed to whole new lifestyle away at college, that his friends haven't changed one bit. They were still trying to hustle their way through life and tried to convince this young brother he was still one of them. This kid didn't forget where he came from, he just knew deep down he was no longer one of them. What his friends failed to realize and understand what he was all about; they couldn't comprehend that he wanted something better out of life and wanted to use his knowledge and wisdom to get it. His friends felt he had changed because he was no longer a part of their street life and still tried to throw him back into their dead end scene. But in the end, the guy wouldn't let his friends control him and began preaching to them about unity, and when you hurt your brother, you're hurting your sister, when you hurt your father, you're hurting your mother, and when you hurt me, you're only hurting yourself. Check yourself.

    This story is all too familiar to me because one of my nephews named Dwayne LaShawn Phoenix had his life taken away from him tragically as a result of gang violence in the ghetto. He was only 17 at the time and his life was taken by a 15 year old boy... *a boy!* Dwayne never got the chance to experience some of the beautiful things that life has to offer him—a higher level of education, a career, children, living life to its fullest. The young brothers out there living dangerously are getting younger and younger every day, taking each others lives, are forgetting one very important thing; they are the next generation. They are the ones who will plant the seed for the generations to come so we can keep the Black race going strong. That means not only just making babies, but taking the responsibility as a man and raising our children and educating them about the ways of the world. Who knows, they may be the next Nobel Prize winner, the next Supreme Court Justice, the next President of the United States. It is time to join together and unite as a people, as one, so that there will be a prophecy for our future generations.

I strongly feel that if my nephew Dwayne had a strong Black father figure is his life, and a strong mother to guide him, maybe he wouldn't have gone down the wrong path. My mother, Dwayne's grandmother, practically raised him by herself because his mother, my sister Jackie, wasn't there like she should have been, in his life. When Jackie became of age and decided to live her life for herself, she chose the wrong lifestyle. Unfortunately, she was also a young mother at the time and didn't live up to her responsibilities as a parent. She was too busy running the streets and doing drugs to care about raising her children. It's very disheartening because not only did she ruin her own life, but she basically ruined the lives of Dwayne and his younger siblings. Dwayne's youngest sister, my niece, was adopted at birth by another woman due to my sister Jackie's substance abuse and not providing a stable home environment for her family. Dwayne, his 2 sisters and 1 brother were also put through the Foster Care system on more than one occasion because Jackie was strung out on drugs and wasn't taking care of her kids. She lost her youngest daughter permanently to the Child Welfare System because she couldn't prove herself to be a fit mother. She fell victim to a plague, a Black Plague that wreaked havoc across the country... and that plague is called "Crack." Crack, the street name for a form of cocaine so addictive, one "hit" changed the face of America. It not only took control of the young people at the time, it also took control of adults; mothers, fathers, sisters, and brothers. It's not a *Black* thing or a *White* thing, it's a *Death* thing. It was a new drug, unlike heroin, that took over your mind and body, it was like the Body Snatchers, if you slept, you became one of them... and I didn't sleep! But what's happening here in America, people need to join together as a nation to really see and hear *what's going on*, the poetic words of the legendary Marvin Gaye's song, "What's Going On" and learn the meaning of "Wake Up Everybody," by Harold Melvin and the Bluenotes. Crack was not only out in the streets, for some of us, it hit home.

My sister Jackie's "crack" habit got so out of hand, she let the drugs take total control of her and made her do one of the most foolish and sinful things she has ever done and will regret for the rest of her life. One Saturday night, Jackie went to my mother's house and my father was there with her, along with some of my siblings. I was performing that night at a club in New York. My father, Frank, was enjoying one of his typical weekend visits with the family, reminiscing to his oldies but goodies on the stereo. My father was the type of man that would lecture you if he felt you were doing something wrong with your life, especially if you were hurting yourself and innocent people. So as usual, when Jackie arrived, obviously under the influence, my father began preaching to her about getting her life together and taking care of her children, his grandchildren. Their discussion turned into a heated verbal dispute between the two of them and the rest of the family tried to calm them down and ease the mounting tension. One thing led to another and within moments, Jackie had pulled out a handgun and shot my father! He was pronounced dead on Sunday, March 22, 1987.

When I came home after my show, in the wee hours of the morning, my wife, Kristine, had to break the horrible news to me. My body just froze when I heard what had happened and I felt a numbness through my veins that just sent chills through every inch of me. I was in a *state of shock*. My family immediately notified the authorities and Jackie was later prosecuted and convicted of this hideous, sinful crime. It has taken my brothers and sisters and me many years to cope with this situation and we still comfort one another about our grief. **How could she?!** It has been a long healing process and has taken everyone in the family several years to come to terms with my sister Jackie, some longer than others, yet it has not been easy for us at all. But to take the life of the man who gave life to you, that fed, bathed, and nurtured you, raised you and taught you right from wrong, tried to help you when you didn't want to help yourself, how could you take his life away?! My mother came real close to doing it on more than one occasion.

My mother, as I previously explained, was always instigating arguments with my father for whatever ridiculous reason she had at the time, and twist and distort it into a fight. And once she started rolling full force with it, out came the insulting remarks about my father's deceased mother, my grandmother, who passed away before I was born. Apparently, my grandmother never liked my mother, and she knew it, and would throw it up in my father's face, adding fuel to the fire every time they fought. But no, she didn't stop there—my mother had to pull out the gun that she kept hidden in the house! Oh yeah, she would try to provoke him or dare him to hit her. And the more he didn't do, the more angry she got! She would pull out that gun in front of the family, friends, even her own grandchildren, not caring who's around that could possibly get hurt. One time I'll never forget, my mother just got so out of hand with her behavior, my father finally tried to put a stop to it and take the gun away from her. She was playing bad-ass with him and tussled with him because she didn't want him to take the gun from her. Sure enough, that gun went off in the struggle, with some of her grandchildren in the room, and *thank God*, no one was injured. It gives me chills every time I think about that incident, and I was just 12 years old at the time, yet my mother carried on with her disturbing behavior until the day my father passed on. I always thought that my mother would have been the fateful one to pull the trigger on my father, but it was his daughter, Jackie, the one who looks and acts the most like my mother, that ended his life. But in all honesty, if Jackie was not the one, it probably would have been my mother. How sad it may be for me to say that, but it's true.

    I miss my father dearly and often feel his presence in my life, especially when I'm listening to my music. One of my favorite Jackson Five songs that always reminds me of my father and brings tears to my eyes is "To Make My Father Proud." I know how proud he was of me, watching me do my MJ thing all the time, but he was a proud father of all his children. He was always there for us, for whatever we needed, even though he didn't live with us full time; he spent every weekend with us and enjoyed singing and dancing with his family to his favorite 45's! Whenever I hear two of my father's favorite songs, "Never Can Say Goodbye" and "I Wanna Be Where Your Are," I picture myself dancing with my father, standing on his feet, as he twirled me around and around, and I cry.

    It's been a long and winding road, but since Jackie was released from prison, she's been battling with herself and putting the pieces of her life back together. She has maintained a family life for herself and her 3 children, less her youngest who was permanently adopted, and has done her best to stay on the right track. God willing, she won't get sidetracked.

CHAPTER 21
Never Can Say Goodbye

The "Dancingest" Jackson, Marlon Jackson, released his long awaited solo album entitled, *Baby Tonight*, featuring the hits, "Don't Go," "Talk 2 U," and the title cut, "Baby Tonight." The music was definitely 80's Pop with an R & B groove, and a touch of Jackson for spice, but the music was his own creation. Marlon wrote, produced, and arranged everything on this album and I am so proud of his work. Of course I love to see the Jacksons work together, but sometimes I like to see them do their own solo thing where their individuality gleams through.

Marlon, the Jackson brother that stands to Tito's left and Jackie's right on stage, is the force, along with Jackie, representing the power that the Jacksons have on stage. I watched Marlon perform on every major music and late night talk show on television, everything from MTV, VH1, to "Soul Train," to "Arsenio Hall," and he has blown me away every time with his dance moves! It is clear to see that dancing is in Marlon's soul and he's proven himself as an outstanding performer. He pours every ounce of blood and sweat in his body into his performance and you literally get tired just watching him. You can't help but smile when you see him perform because he is a true showman. During the Victory Tour, Marlon not only did his individual part as a Jackson brother, but was a backup to Michael and absent brother Jackie throughout the tour! Quite a feat that most couldn't handle and handle well, like Marlon. To me he is extremely talented and is often overshadowed by his other brothers. Many people may not know this, but Marlon co-starred in the made-for-TV movie entitled, *Student Confidential*, and he also wrote a song for the motion picture, *The Golden Child*, starring Eddie Murphy. It's a shame to say it but Marlon's album had so much potential, it really should have been much more successful than it was. He worked extremely hard on this album and didn't receive the credit that was due to him. Marlon is so full of energy, he should get an "A+" for effort alone.

Just like my brother Steven, who was also so full of energy and life. He loved to tease and *torture* me endlessly, just to piss me off. Steven was very smart—a real math wizard that could tackle any problem or equation, and I would often turn to him for help with my homework, since math was not my best subject. He also loved sports, all sports, and could sit in front of the TV all day and watch game after game after game... football, basketball, baseball, boxing, just like my father. Steven was a loyal fan and admirer of Smokey Robinson and The Miracles and would always get up and sing his favorite songs when the family was gathered around the living room, "Doggone Right," "Tears of a Clown," and "Ooo Baby Baby." And when Smokey Robinson left The Miracles, he was deeply affected by it and didn't know what he would do after the group broke up, just like I didn't know what I would do when Jermaine left the Jackson Five. My brother Steven was the biggest Smokey Robinson and The Miracles fan, just as I was the biggest Jackson Five fan.

But on December 31, 1987, New Year's Eve, tragedy had struck my family again right in the same apartment that my father's life was taken away by a handgun, controlled by the thing that I consider to be the "Grim Reaper"... drugs. This poison had also taken my brother Steven's life, but by his own doing and abuse of these substances. For years, just like my sister Jackie, my whole family tried to beg and plead with Steven to leave the drugs alone. He was too smart for that and should have known better. At one point in his life, our family had forced him into rehab, with surprising success, and saw him come out clean and take control of his own life, but not for long... Maybe we were fooling ourselves thinking Steven would learn from his mistakes and get on with his life on the right track. But what a slap in the face it was to have him come out of rehab and go right back into the same street environment to the same place where his same friends were doing the same stupid thing! Voices of evil spirits were calling him and there lied temptation and he was too weak to refuse it. *Mercy, mercy me, what's going on* with those *inner city blues*? Steven was living in every word of these songs because these songs are reality. He was back on the drug merry-go-round again, going round and round, on a ride to nowhere, finding himself lost in the sky with diamonds. And on December 31, 1987, before the clock could strike 12:00 to welcome in the New Year, in this amusement park where his friends and family were, Steven took his final ride on the merry-go-round and bought his stairway to heaven through a drug overdose.

It makes me so damn mad to see adults and children abuse their bodies and lives in such a way with this poison that they're literally inviting death upon their doorstep. Death finds us all sooner or later, but it's not dying that's important, it's how you die. My father's death was untimely; he died before his time and it shook me up so badly I could not believe what had happened. To me it felt like a bad dream, a nightmare, that I could awake from and everything would be okay... but it wasn't. But my brother Steven's death was more real because he had control of his *destiny* and made the wrong choice. And when he died, a piece of me died along with him. The blood that flows through me as well as my father also flowed through him. I feel that since we were born of the same parents, had the same blood and came from the same womb, we, all of my siblings, are one of the same. But I guess the whole scenario is just like the story in the Bible about Cain and Abel... and I had to come to terms that I am not my brother's keeper. And whenever I listen to Smokey's music or any other Motown artist's music, I reminisce about the days when my family used to spend time together playing our favorite 45 records on the stereo hi-fi, dancing and singing with one another, and I think of Steven pretending to be Smokey Robinson.

CHAPTER 22

Happy

With the release of *Bad*, Michael Jackson had to prove he really was *bad* as he embarked upon his first solo world tour without his brothers by his side. Michael's Bad World Tour began in Japan, September 1987, where he was received like royalty by the Japanese. The tour then traveled internationally for several months and finally made its way to the United States. On February 23, 1988, Michael kicked off his 1st American solo tour in Kansas City, Missouri, just like opening night of the Victory Tour, July 6, 1984. The spectacular tour spanned over 16 months around the world, ending with 5 sold out concerts in Los Angeles, California. All eyes were on him as people wanted to see if Michael could kick it live all by himself... and he did! His solo effort was definitely *BAD* and worthy of a standing ovation because Michael proved his ability to hold an entire concert alone without his brothers, after performing with them for almost 2 decades! With Michael's talent, stage presence, and professionalism, it was quite an admirable feat to have total control of a concert and not have to rely on his brothers as a back up for anything! Being the perfectionist that he is, Michael never would have attempted this tour without having complete confidence in himself that he could go solo successfully.

The tour itself was as grandiose as the Victory Tour, except without all the ridiculous hype. I saw the Bad Tour at Madison Square Garden in New York on March 5, 1988 and was as equally impressed by Michael's presentation as I was by the Victory Tour's. The elaborate staging was state of the art equipment, clearly displayed at the beginning of the show. A giant computerized screen, consistently of thousands and thousands of lights that formed an animated image of MJ's feet walking across the screen and the digitalized sound effects of his footsteps. The image then began to "Moonwalk" across the screen, stops, does a spin, and then goes up on his toes with a **BBBBAAAAAMMMMMM!!!!** sound effect so intense you can feel it in your gut! The power of the bright lights and the thunderous sound effects gave me a fabulous rush as the computerized screen slowly rose into the air, only to reveal the King of Pop himself. Michael came from beneath the stage and paused for a moment to give his band members and 4 backup dancers a cue that it was time to show the world ***Who's Bad***!!

    His opening number, "Wanna Be Startin' Somethin'" was the perfect intro to his solo show, proving that he was ready for the world. The band then flowed right into "Heartbreak Hotel" as the crowd screamed with excitement. "Heartbreak Hotel" was not only a Jackson song from their *Triumph* album, it was Michael's artistic creation, as it was written, arranged and composed by him. The song's driving beats and Michael's dance movements, which resemble an Indian tribal rain dance, collaborate into a beautiful ceremonious display. Throughout the concert Michael performed a compilation of hit songs from his multi-million selling albums, *Off The Wall*, *Thriller*, and *Bad*, such as "Rock With You," "She's Out Of My Life," "Working Day And Night," "Beat It," "Billie Jean," "Human Nature," "Smooth Criminal," "Another Part Of Me," "The Way You Make Me Feel," and many more. What was really great for this tour was that it was the first time Michael performed the title song from his record-breaking, chart-topping, #1 selling over 40 million copies and still counting album in the *history* of music... *Thriller*! Michael amazed the audience with a magical illusion during this song, where he went off to stage right into a small tent already propped up on stage. As he entered this tent, the accompanying horror music set the haunting mood. The tent was opaque, but you could see Michael's silhouette inside, as he was undergoing his transformation. He emerged from the tent with the monstrous head of the infamous werewolf, big hairy hands, and varsity letterman's jacket with his initials on it, just like in the *Thriller* video. Michael slowly crept across the stage like an animal stalking his prey and then re-entered the tent and went into a frenzy, fighting to get out. All of a sudden, the tent collapsed, leaving no trace of Michael in sight. At the same precise time, Michael reappeared at the opposite side of the stage, still in his monster mask, as the pyrotechnical effects exploded, adding to the illusion.

Michael performed "Thriller" a la werewolf with his backup dancers dressed as ghoulish monsters, just like the video itself. They even did the famous "Thriller" dance routine as the lights went out and Michael's jacket lit up the stage. And they couldn't do "Thriller" without the legendary King of Horror, Vincent Price, and his thrilling rap. It was great!! And for some strange reason it just isn't the same without that haunting voice of Vincent Price and his fiendish laugh at the end. The audience was spellbound by it all.

Throughout the entire concert, Michael razzled and dazzled his fans with his electrifying moves, awesome lights and effects, and magical illusions. It was a fabulous stage show that grossed over $125 million worldwide in 5 continents, selling out all over the world in numerous countries. In all honesty, Michael has never ceased to amaze me with his talent. There's no better way to describe it, but Michael has pure, raw, God-given talent, and that is something that no one can buy or acquire because it is a true gift. And the one thing that I admire most about Michael is that he never stops dreaming. He has a hunger for performing that hasn't been fed yet because he still yearns for more and more. But Michael doesn't just dream, he makes his dreams a reality each and every day as he reaches for the stars, higher and higher. And if he is living in a fantasy world that is called Never Never Land, then may he never never leave!

With the success of *Bad*, my career once again took flight and I was soaring above the clouds. I had to update my costumes and grow my hair into a really long jheri curl, to stay a cut above. And let me tell you, long hair is bad enough, but a long jheri curl, that shit was a project just trying to maintain it. I had to keep it tied in a ponytail during my off days for my own sanity. Ah, what some of us do for the price of fame!

Since Michael was really hot, I was out on the road performing once again, doing the *Bad* thing, dancing to some new music. Of course every where I went now, all I heard was "Who's bad, Michael?" and "Are you bad?" and "Hee hee hee!" Everybody's a comedian. But I wasn't complaining; everything was going great, until tragedy struck again. June 1988 I lost my brother Bruce, the biggest prankster in the family. He was always joking with people and teasing them; couldn't get enough of it. Bruce always believed in keeping the family bond strong, but the separation between him and his wife and his only son, caused him great pain. He began drinking as a way of coping with this situation and easing the pain, and frankly, never stopped. He became an alcoholic, especially after the death of my father and then my brother Steven. Bruce and

Steven were like best friends and used to do everything together. They were inseparable, kind of like joined at the hip, and when Steven died, half of Bruce died. And it almost seemed like he just gave up on life after that because only months later, Bruce died himself. Because I was out on the road a lot during this time, I was under the assumption that Bruce died of cirrhosis of the liver. But my siblings and I always thought there was more to the story with Bruce's death that our mother kept from us. We all thought that since Bruce and Steven were so close, he just could not live without him, and my father, too. Of course he and Steven were very close to our father and the three of them would get together to watch different sports all the time... you know that male bonding stuff. It's a beautiful thing to really love your family that much, usually it's a husband and wife that can't live without the other spouse when one dies. But in this case, it's a son and a brother. I really miss those two even though they used to gang up on me all the time.

After the last service for Bruce at the funeral home, I found myself, instead of going to his burial site with the rest of my family, walking around the neighborhood for a while. Something spiritual led me to my old elementary school, P.S. 3 in Bedford-Stuyvesant section of Brooklyn, New York and when I walked into the school, I had an overwhelming feeling of wanting to give something back to my school. I approached the principal, Ms. Poindexter, and offered to do a show at the school to help them raise money to buy books and other educational supplies that the children needed. It was indeed fate that drew me there because as luck would have it, they were planning to have their annual talent show and Ms. Poindexter took me into the school auditorium to show me the decorations they had already put up. Just seeing the auditorium again took me back to yesteryear and I was reminiscing about the roar of the crowd back in 1974 when I performed on that same stage during their annual talent show. I performed the Jackson Five's then #1 hit, "Dancin' Machine" and stole the whole show!

Ms. Poindexter said it would be a pleasure to have me come back and perform, but I said the pleasure would be all mine to give something back to the school and also send a message to the children to follow their dreams because dreams really do come true. As I continued to walk through the school, I ran into my teacher, Mrs. McNeil, who recognized me immediately as she yelled my name down the hall. The first thing she said to me was, "Do you remember what I taught you?" and I said "Yes." And like dejá vu, she grabbed me by the hand and took me through the school to proudly show me off as one of her star pupils to all the other teachers. Some I remembered from when I attended years ago and some were newcomers. Mrs. McNeil explained to all of them how she was a grown woman arguing with this nine year old kid about how important it is to get an education. One of her most famous quotes was "A mind is a terrible thing to waste." While we were conversing about the good old days when I was a young student, in came my 5th grade teacher, Mrs. Barbara Hairston. I felt like God had brought her to me because if there really are angels here on earth, then Mrs. Hairston is definitely one of them. She truly is God-sent for all the children that she has taught in her lifetime of being a teacher. She is the most caring, motherly, generous, kindest, sweetest, spiritual woman that I've ever known. What this world needs is more teachers like her because teachers are not getting the respect they deserve and are highly underpaid for their efforts. Mrs. Hairston is the perfect role model for anyone aspiring to become a teacher.

She would take time out with her students individually to see that they were getting the proper attention they needed to learn. Mrs. Hairston took me into her classroom and introduced me to her students by saying, in her words, "These are my children" as if they really were her children. She had a special love for each and every one of them, as she had for each and every one of her children she's had over the years in her classroom. She told her children that "this is a student of mine that will always be a child of mine" and that I was someone that followed my dreams and achieved them. She used me as an example to her students by stressing that you are somebody and can grow up to be whatever you wish, if you believe in yourself. I felt so much love and adoration coming from Mrs. Hairston as I always have had love and admiration for her. It seemed that years gone by was only a day's time in our lives. From that day on, we have remained close, like a mother and son, and she has always been there for me when I needed that spiritual inspiration and faith. We often pray together over the phone or in person, and it still is a ritual between us. She is the one who helped me become "saved" and to accept Jesus Christ as my sole saviour.

    The following week was the Big Show and I felt like a kid anxiously waiting to get out on the stage and perform. I was so excited about the show that when I was waiting to go on standing backstage before the curtains opened, I felt like I was 10 years old again! Well show time came and I hit the stage like *dynamite*! I had to do one of my favorite Jackson medleys, "Wanna Be Startin' Somethin'," "Another Part Of Me," "Billie Jean," and "Shake Your Body (Down To The Ground)" for the standing room only crowd at the school! Never in all my days of attending this school did I see any of my teachers let their hair down and have a good time... until then! Everyone, including teachers, students, parents, and the principal were dancing in the aisles having a good ol' time! When I took my bows, the thunderous applause and cheers of happiness and love were music to my ears. It was one of the most beautiful sounds I've ever heard because *I let sadness see what happy does, and let happy be what sadness was.*

CHAPTER 23
2300 Jackson Street

Talk about being in the right place at the right time, that's how I met Jackie Jackson. Right in the reception area of Polygram Records, his record label, is where we were introduced, in May of 1989. I was stunned and almost speechless and I couldn't believe I was standing face to face with a member of one of the world's most famous families, Jackie Jackson of the renowned Jacksons! He was in town promoting his new album release entitled, *Be The One*, for Polygram Records. It was such an honor to meet him because I've been a fan for so many years that I had to get his autograph! I missed him when I went to the Jacksons' sound check for the Victory Tour in 1984 because he was recovering from knee surgery and wasn't traveling to every city with his brothers.

As Jackie and I made our way down the elevator to exit the building, we spoke of many things dealing with the music industry and the Jackson family. He also let me in on a little hush-hush industry information that the Jacksons were putting the finishing touches on their soon-to-be released album, *2300 Jackson Street*, while he was enjoying the beautiful city of New York. We exited the building together onto 7th Avenue and proceeded to walk from 52nd Street to 57th Street with his bodyguard in tow. There was a limousine waiting for him with another security guard inside, but Jackie insisted on walking because he said it was such a beautiful spring day. During our walk together, I asked him what it takes to maintain the longevity of success his family has had for so many years and his reply was "...to believe in yourself... hard work, determination, and to have positive people in your corner... everything else comes easy." I also asked him how his knee had been recuperating after the surgery he had prior to the Victory Tour, since he was sidelined from the whole tour. He said his knee was doing fine but that will be one tour he'll always remember because he was so hurt that he couldn't perform with his brothers. He said after working with his brothers for so many years together it was like playing for the home team in the World Series and you're sitting on the sidelines while the rest of the team gets to play. As we continued to walk, Jackie started snacking on a bag of roasted peanuts with some hard butterscotch candy, I guess trying to make his own honey roasted effect, and offered some to me, but I declined. He asked me my opinion of his new album, since I told him I was such an admirer of him and his family, and I eagerly told him that I thought it was great and I looked forward to seeing some videos from the album. "Cruisin'" was already a hit in the clubs and "Stuck On You" was being played on New York's WBLS's "Quiet Storm" program, which features a variety of R & B love ballads. Jackie also spoke of his family and how proud he was of his brothers and sisters as he was on his way to visit his sister, LaToya, who was living in New York City at the time, in the Galleria Building on 57th Street.

As we parted company on 57th Street, I felt like I had known Jackie all my life because he was so comfortable speaking to me—a stranger he trusted as a friend. He was very open and honest with me and I'll always remember him for his kindness and knowledgeable advice.

Another celebrity I literally stumbled upon was Prince, in August 1987 in New York. My wife and I went to see the

Broadway hit show, *Starlight Express*, and arrived at the theater five minutes after the show began. You never can depend on the subways to get you there on time! One of the ushers escorted us into the theater to find our seats, and as we walked up the side aisle, which was very dark, we stumbled right over a man that was sitting on the dark staircase. He was wearing a red suit, leaning his chin on the walking stick he holding in front of him as a chin rest. Not realizing who he was just yet, my wife, Kristine, whispered to me "there's another one who thinks he's Prince." I chuckled thinking to myself that this man here must really think he's Prince with his flashy red tuxedo suit, his gold tipped walking stick, and his wavy black hair. We apologized to the man for practically stepping on him and he politely excused himself and said "Excuse me, I'm sorry" and then nodded his head in acceptance of our apology. We then took our seats about 5 chairs down from where "he" was sitting and glanced over at the man on the stairs one more time. It was then that we both noticed 2 large bodyguards— one at the top of the stairs and the other at the bottom of the stairs, obviously not your average theater ushers. There was no doubt that this really was Prince sitting just 6 feet away from us. What luck! Being the fan and admirer that I am of his music and his stage performance, I *had* to ask him for his autograph. Hey, the opportunity may never come around again! So I got out of my seat and walked right over to him and within seconds, his bodyguards were **right there**, just as a precaution. I said that I was sorry to disturb him, but could I please have an autograph since I was such an admirer of his craft and his music. Prince seemed *happy* to oblige, but I didn't have a pen handy, and neither did he. Smart move, right? After searching our pockets for a few moments and feeling dumbfounded, Prince smiled and graciously said "I'm sorry I would love sign it, but neither one of us have a pen... how about we wait until the show is over and I'll sign it for you then?" I told him it would be no problem at all and thanked him for his time. I went back to my seat to watch the play, anxiously waiting 'til the end of the performance, but somehow about 10 minutes before intermission, Prince quietly exited stage left before the lights came up so he could get out safely without anyone seeing him. I understood his early departure because sometimes you have to pay the price of fame by never getting to see an entire play, concert, movie, etc. from start to finish. It's all for security reasons. And needless to say, I still haven't had the opportunity to meet with him again and get an autograph from the Artist formerly known as Prince.

1989 was like dejá vu of the year 1973 for the Jacksons when three members of the group had solo albums out the same time the group's album was out. Huh?! Let me explain—in 1973, three of the Jackson brothers had released their solo albums; Michael's *Music In Me*, Jermaine's *Come Into My Life*, and Jackie's *Jackie*, all during the same year as the Jackson Five's albums, *Skywriter* and *Get It Together* were released. Nothing like cornering the market! And again in 1989, three of the brothers had solo releases; Jermaine's *Don't Take It Personal*, Jackie's *Be The One*, and Randy's *Randy & The Gypsies*, along with the Jacksons' *2300 Jackson Street*!! Now that's mass marketing at its finest!

Jermaine's album, *Don't Take It Personal* was his best album to date, edging out over his 1986 album, *Precious Moments*. *Precious Moments* had crossed Jermaine over with a commercialized Pop sound, but *Don't Take It Personal* was a more solid R & B sound that could have been used for a motion picture soundtrack, particularly the ballad, "Words Into Action" where Jermaine uses his extraordinary melodic vocals, emulating one of his favorite singers, the late great Marvin Gaye. Another great tune from the album is the hit, "If You Say My Eyes Are Beautiful," the duet with Whitney Houston. Jermaine and Whitney also teamed up for "Take Good Care Of My Heart" from Jermaine's 1984 *Dynamite* album and "Nobody Loves Me Like You Do" from Whitney's debut album, *Whitney*, in 1984. Jermaine and Whitney also performed this song live on the daytime soap opera, "As The World Turns." And acting, well he's done that, too, co-starring with Pia Zadora in the film, *Voyage of the Rock Aliens*, 1988. Jermaine even expanded his musical talents into movie soundtracks, including, but not limited to, two songs from the movie *Perfect*, starring Jamie Lee Curtis and John Travolta, the theme song "Closest Thing To Perfect" and "Shock Me," another duet with Whitney Houston. He also contributed the song "All Revved Up" to the motion picture *Beverly Hills Cop II*, starring Eddie Murphy, 1987, and the song "Clean Up Your Act" for the *I'm Gonna Git You Sucka* movie soundtrack, starring, written and directed by Keenan Ivory Wayans, in 1988. But soundtracks aren't just Jermaine's territory; brother Jackie also made waves with his title cut "Be The One" for the motion picture *My Stepmother Is An Alien*, starring Dan Ackroyd and Kim Basinger, and two tracks for *The Running Man*, in 1987, starring Arnold Schwarzenegger—"Paula's Theme" and "The Death March." Even the Jacksons had to get in on the action with "Time Out," the theme song for *Burglar*, starring Whoopi Goldberg, in 1987. It pays to read those boring credits at the end of the next movie you see; you may find a Jackson song listed!

    I didn't mean to sidetrack with the soundtracks, but *Don't Take It Personal* is a timeless classic collection of songs that you never get tired of listening to. The biggest hits from the album were "Two Ships," "I'd Like To Get To Know You," and the title cut, "Don't Take It Personal." This album not only expressed love, but it's also perfect for those lovemaking times, just like some of the world's most famous artists who wrote the book on the art of lovemaking; Marvin Gaye, Teddy Pendergrass, Barry White, Julio Iglesias, and others, whose music has spread love everywhere. Jermaine deserves to be recognized in this category also. They all are the maestros of love.

Jermaine did a worldwide promotion of his album because of its success internationally. Predominantly every radio station whose format was Adult Contemporary or R & B/Soul was playing different songs from this album, along with the music video networks showing his videos every day. Jermaine even hit the talk show circuit, performing live on some of them, which was a rare treat for his fans. Jermaine was not only busy with his own promotional tour, he was also tied up promoting the Jacksons' *2300 Jackson Street* album with his brothers, Tito, Jackie and Randy, at the same time. The four Jackson brothers hit every corner of the market promoting this album... TV shows, clubs, record stores, etc., in every corner of the world! It was hot! *2300 Jackson Street* is definitely one of their masterpiece albums to date, along with their chart-topping blockbuster album, *Triumph*, from 1980. Their 1984 *Victory* album had all 6 brothers taking lead, writing, producing and performing their own songs on the album, but *2300 Jackson Street* was the album that proved the Jacksons, as a group, could survive without Michael Jackson. This album is a creative collaboration of the four brothers, Jermaine, Tito, Jackie, and Randy, which included the entire Jackson clan, including the grandchildren, except for sister LaToya, participating on the title cut, "2300 Jackson Street."

2300 Jackson Street represents love and family unity. The

title is cleverly named from the actual street address where the Jacksons resided in Gary, Indiana when they first became the Jackson Five. This album also marks the Jacksons' 25th anniversary as the biggest, most successful family group in the recording industry from 1964-1989. It was a gift in tribute to their parents Joseph and Katherine Jackson, who without them, all this would not be possible. I personally would like to commend Joe & Katherine Jackson for raising nine beautiful children, Rebbie, Jackie, Tito, Jermaine, LaToya, Marlon, Michael, Randy, and Janet, drug free, in an urban environment, and creating the world famous Jackson family that people all across the globe have come to love and adore. Thank you, Joseph and Katherine Jackson, *"you are the ones!"*

The first hit from *2300 Jackson Street*, "Nothin' (That Compares 2 U)," was written and produced by L.A. Reid and Babyface, two of the hottest writers and producers in the music industry. The song had a fresh, modern sound created by L.A. & Babyface with the Jacksons' flavor, and their perfect harmonizing vocals that were reminiscent of the original Jackson sound that never died. To this day, you still hear the Jacksons famous sound influencing many top recording artists of today and yesteryear. Many artists have tried to duplicate the Jacksons' sound and even the traditional Jackson Five sound, with groups like the Osmonds (remember them?), the Sylvers, and the DeFrancos. They were the 70's copycat version of the J5 who tried to cash in on a hot new musical sound created by the Jackson Five, "Bubble gum" music, and cater it to the White kids, except for the Sylvers. By the mid 80's, groups like New Edition, Menudo, Five Star, and New Kids on the Block, tried to emulate the Jackson Five with their music, dance steps, and even stage costumes, but nobody has come remotely close to the Jackson Five's status in the industry. And now in the 90's, you have different artists sampling music of the Jacksons and the Jackson Five, recycling their sound for a new song. Many legendary innovators in the world of music, such as Sly and the Family Stone, the "Funk-Masters," and "The Godfather of Soul," James Brown, have their music sampled all the time by contemporary artists. The most famous use of a Jackson Five sampling is from their #1 selling hit, "ABC," used in the rap group, Naughty By Nature's hit song, "O.P.P." There are other samplings, as there will continue to be others, as the course of music *history* winds into the future.

"Nothin' (That Compares 2 U)" featured all four brothers taking turns at the lead vocals which was ingenious and it worked well for them. Even the video for the song was great, highlighting the playfulness and "brotherhood" between the brothers. It was one of my favorite cuts from the album, along with "2300 Jackson Street." "2300 Jackson Street," was produced by the Jacksons with Teddy Riley. Teddy is the creative force behind many performing artists, including his first group Guy, which he was a member of, and other top artists like Bobby Brown, Keith Sweat, Tom Jones, and Michael Jackson himself. Teddy Riley's reputation as an innovative producer earned him the title of the Master/Creator of the "New Jack Swing" sound in music which was born in 1988 and is still thriving. L.A. and Babyface began their impressive career in 1987 with the formation of the R & B group, The Deal. L.A. & Face have written and produced for so many artists it has become countless, but some of the most widely recognized artists on their list includes: Aretha Franklin, Barry White, Madonna, Patti LaBelle, Gladys Knight, and Eric Clapton. This dynamic duo has made their mark in music *history* and will continue their creative work for years and years to come, even if they work separately, as they do now.

2300 Jackson Street is a provocative, fresh, even daring sound that will remain timeless for the Jacksons. The first track, "Art Of Madness," with Jackie and Jermaine on lead vocals, is a distinct European sound with a strong driving beat, intermingled with several different mechanical sounds, that became a big hit in Europe, along with the song, "If You'd Only Believe." "If You'd Only Believe" was a smooth ballad that featured Jermaine and Jackie on lead vocals. Why wasn't it a big hit in the U.S.... who knows, (politics?), but I thought the song had a strong crossover appeal. "She," sung by Randy Jackson, produced by Teddy Riley and written by Aaron Hall and Gene Griffin of the group Guy, was a hip-hop, street flavored song, with a dash of the New Jack Swing. This song appealed to a younger audience and was a powerful dance song, but it was never pushed or promoted the way it should have been. Again, we're talking politics in the music industry and sometimes the general public doesn't understand why a song or an album doesn't receive the proper airplay or promotion it deserves. All in all, I think the *2300 Jackson Street* album was great; it was a contemporary collection of Jackson hits, featuring different producers who offered their musical flair, but never taking away that distinct Jackson flavor, only enhancing it.

Randy Jackson, the youngest and most versatile musician of the Jackson brothers was also venturing into the solo zone! For years Randy desired to do his own music, ever since he recorded his first solo hit single for Epic/CBS Records in 1978, "How Can I Be Sure," a love ballad which had only minimal success. Truthfully, if the record company invested a little more time and money into utilizing Randy's talents and abilities as a solo artist, he would have had comparable success to Jermaine and Michael, but for whatever reason they didn't.

Randy's new album, entitled, *Randy & The Gypsies*, went far beyond what the public and fans expected. For the album, Randy recruited the best, raw, talented musicians he could find to produce the new "Gypsies" sound he wanted to create. The album is pure genius; it is an excellent musical concept and a collaboration of Funk, Jazz, Soul, R & B, Hip-Hop, and Pop music, all rolled into one. The musical sounds and styles on this album are so unique and diverse that most people, even avid Jackson fans, didn't know that it was Randy Jackson, one of the world famous Jackson brothers. This musician extraordinaire is the same little 10 year old kid that joined his brothers, the Jackson Five, on his first TV appearance on the variety show, "Hell's A Poppin'," where he performed his bongo solo and captured the hearts of millions. It was clear to see then that there was a lot more to come from this budding little musician, who was a member of the multi-talented Jackson family.

The album, *Randy & The Gypsies*, featured the hit songs "Perpetrators," "Love You Honey," and the ballad, "The Love We Almost Had." But what I really admire Randy for is that he completely detracted from anything Jackson-looking, Jackson-sounding, with this album and did his own music without using his Jackson name. It was an opportunity for Randy to express himself musically without standing in the shadows of his brothers. The album received raved reviews from several music critics and top industry musicians for its arrangements and production. Even big brother Jackie said that he liked his sister Janet's *Rhythm Nation 1814* album, "but Randy's is better." Jackie, the oldest brother, is so proud of his family, especially his brothers and sisters, even sister LaToya admitted that no one is prouder of the family than Jackie is. Jackie speaks so highly of his family for their individual efforts and group successes, and allows himself to step away from them and look upon them as a stranger, and recognize and praise them for their talents and achievements as if he wasn't a part of them. His sincerity and warmth when he speaks of his family just shines right through as you can read the truthfulness and love in his eyes. He's his own family's best fan!

All united, and standing strong, and still today, they're one big family.

CHAPTER 24
We've Got Forever

1991 was a beautiful time in my life, but yet sorrowful as well. This was the year that God blessed me with another angel, my daughter, Timanda. She was a child that came out of wedlock to a woman I had no ties to, no commitments to. It was at a time in my career that I was busy with my travels when I was preyed upon by a woman that had no good intentions, only but for herself. But being an entertainer, someone of celebrity status, you are always being preyed upon by some obsessive fan, stalker, or extortioner. I, as a man, let my guards down and should have been thinking with my intellectual mind, knowledge and wisdom that God has granted me with, instead of my stupid head. And this mistake I made was a lesson to be learned. Not only did I make the wrong decision, but I hurt someone else along the way; a woman that means the most to me, a woman that has stuck by my side *through thick and thin*, 'cause *she's good* to me. What I believe about a woman is the more you give, the more you receive; if you give her a house, she'll return a home; if you give her food, she'll return a meal; if you give her your seed, she'll return an angel from heaven... and that my wife, Kristine, has provided for me and made it all possible. But this child that I had from a brief affair, I love unconditionally, despite the circumstances. The minute I was told this woman had conceived my child, I loved this child instantly. But I faced one of the most difficult tasks I've ever had to do in my life; breaking the news to my wife. It caused a lot of friction between us, but not to the point of us screaming at the top of our lungs to each other. The worst *torture* for me was living in silence with her; it was like living in a tomb where the quietness had gotten loud. She didn't lose her self-respect, she didn't try to hurt me or make me feel less than a man; she remained just like a lady 'til the end. And as time went by, we have grown far beyond closer than we ever were in our lives together, as she gave me *one more chance*. After going through this ordeal with my wife, I've dedicated a song to her as a symbol in building a stronger relationship together, even though our union was already strong. The song I dedicate to Kristine is sung by Smokey Robinson and the Miracles entitled, "We've Come Too Far To End It Now," from their *Flying High Together* album. Kristine and I have come too far in our lives together to end it now due to a mistake I made, even though I am still repenting for that mistake. She learned to forgive me and we put it all behind us, moving ahead in the positive direction. From the moment Kristine laid eyes on my daughter, she loved and accepted her as one of her own, with the same love and affection she has for my two sons, and we were *flying high together* once again. A symbol for all we have accomplished together, building our lives together, reaching for the stars, our dreams together, is the Smokey Robinson and the Miracles' album entitled, *Flying High Together*. We flew above and beyond the dark clouds and into the heavens again, and that's by taking it *one heartbeat* at a time.

    The birth of our son, Frank Dwayne, born in December 1992, was perhaps a blessing in disguise. He was also the angel sent to me by God that strengthened my will to persevere, along with a multitude of prayers and support from my friends and family. I was going through purgatory on earth with my daughter's mother at the time. She was obsessed, out of control, and would not accept the fact the she couldn't have me in her life for what she wanted me to be. Yes, I wanted to be a father to Timanda more than anything in this world, but not under her conditions. I could not and would not make any commitments to her and for that, she made my life a living hell because I wanted no part of her, only my daughter. So she played my daughter like a game of chess against me, using every move, every strategy, to win, and Timanda was her "King" that I had to capture. But the game got too complicated and in time I was forced to surrender, waving my white flag in defeat. One thing I do know, is that Jesus has always carried me through the storm.

    Frank Dwayne, born December 9, 1992, was named after my father, Frank, and my nephew, Dwayne, who have both passed on. Little Frank is the continuing legacy of the Phoenix name and had to be rightfully named in honor of his grandfather and cousin. And he came out with a bang, only three weeks early, because his actual due date was December 31, New Years Eve! From the minute I saw him in his first sonogram, I knew he was going to be a boy with his long skinny body and big head. So when he came into the world, it was no surprise to me. And of all my children, he is the most like me, as my wife loves to remind me! He's a fast learner, very *happy* and sweet, and full of life! He's also very agile and coordinated, as he shares with me my love of dancing and music, just like my daughter, Timanda. She too is very musically inclined and talented, and loves to be in the "spotlight" and perform! My son Timothy is the master artist and draws just like a Marvel comic book artist, maybe better. Gemaile inherits my kindhearted soul and sensitivity, and loves to watch cartoons, just like me. All my children take a little something from me, but I have to laugh sometimes when I see Frank and Timanda play together. They get along great as brother and sister, but sometimes she would really get on his nerves trying to show off and compete with him. They're both big Michael Jackson fans, and they like to watch his videos and imitate his steps, but at the same time try to outdo one another to see who can dance better! But I never forced Michael Jackson upon them; they discovered him on their own. I guess it's true what many a people have said about Michael; he has a special, magnetic quality about himself that children just love and adore, and my two youngest children are no exceptions. As young as they are, they really get into their performance and even do all the facial expressions like Michael. And don't forget the fedora hats and their microphone! Gotta have the whole ensemble!

My wife and I always play a large variety of music in our home so our children grew up with listening to the same music that we enjoy. Some of my favorites artists include Al Green, the Jackson Five, Smokey Robinson, and many Motown artists. My son Frank loves the music too, and likes to imitate Smokey Robinson, bopping his head back and forth to the slow groove, even doing his facial expressions, trying to be a little "Smoke!" It's so adorable watching him imitate one of the greats in music *history* because he gets so into his performance, like a real pro. But it makes me proud to see him appreciate and identify real music. As young as he is, he has an amazing ear for music and can identify so many different artists by just hearing their music alone. And he'll tell you too if it's the Jacksons, not the Jackson Five, or if it's Jermaine, not Michael, if it's Smokey, James Brown, or Prince.

Frank also thinks he's a comedian. One day, our neighbor kept asking him what his name was and he finally got so fed up that he just blurted out the name "Tito!" My wife and I laughed hysterically as we asked each other, "Where did that come from?" We're still trying to figure that one out! Then he started telling everyone that asked him, his name was Tito! Frank would always watch a lot of the old Jackson Five clips from different television appearances with me, as well as the old Jackson Five cartoons, and somehow the name "Tito" stuck in his head. Not Michael or Jermaine, but Tito! For the longest time, he was telling everyone his name was Tito, until he suddenly reverted back to Frank one day. Whew!! I was beginning to think that maybe as he got a little older he might want me to change his name to Tito, like I had my mother change my name and add Timothy as my middle name. I don't know, the name *Frank Tito* just doesn't flow right! Besides, there's only room for one "Tito" in this world!

TOUCHED BY THE JACKSONS

CHAPTER 25
The Dream Goes On

As luck would have it, I had the opportunity to meet yet another Jackson—sister LaToya! LaToya was in New York promoting her newly released book, *Growing Up in the Jackson Family*, when I caught up with her. I'm sure we all remember LaToya's shocking "tell all" book about life with her family and the controversy it caused. I don't really want to comment on her book personally, but it was a rebellious move for LaToya, and it brought her the media attention that she desired. Just like when she did her first nude layout for *Playboy* magazine; she certainly caused quite a commotion with her family and the media. Of course everyone was "shocked" over the photos of quiet little LaToya posing nude—how could she, she's a Jackson?! But the media blew it all out of proportion and made it seem like the Jackson family scandal of the century! Frankly, I thought the *Playboy* layout was very tastefully done and LaToya looked very sexy and beautiful. It was like a work of art and LaToya's statuesque body was like a Greek goddess's. But the media just feasts off of controversial or bad press and uses it to their fullest advantage, playing their prey against one another, like they did with LaToya and the Jackson family. The media really took it to the extreme and exploited their power with the Jacksons at every given opportunity. They preyed upon the weak and vulnerable one, LaToya, because I feel she was too naive and inexperienced with the media vultures. The media stepped right in and tried to turn LaToya against her family, the family against LaToya, LaToya against her management, different family members against each other, hoping to catch one or more of them out there, creating a juicy tale of deception, hate, and lies. This is why brother Tito always tells his sons to stick together, foremost as brothers, secondly as performers, and don't let anyone ever get between you. Divide and conquer together, as a family unit, and no one shall be able to break the chain. We all know that being a celebrity, being preyed upon comes with the territory being in the public eye, but when the media literally tries to tear a family apart, they are overstepping their boundaries by far!

LaToya and I met at the ABC-TV studios of "Live! With Regis and Kathie Lee" where she was appearing that day for her book promotion. LaToya was as friendly, sweet, and just as beautiful in person as she looks on television or in photos. It was an honor for me to finally meet one of the famed Jackson sisters face-to-face! And as we walked out of the ABC building together after the taping of the show, we got mobbed by her fans and admirers waiting outside. Everyone swarmed around us like bees to honey, as I noticed LaToya's bodyguard and manager/husband, Jack Gordon, standing right by us as a precaution. There were a lot of guys standing outside waiting for LaToya, holding their copies of the infamous *Playboy* magazine which featured her nude layout. I felt like these hounds were only there to see LaToya "in the flesh"—(they weren't real fans)—and I had to protect her like she was my own sister! I put my arm around her shoulder and whispered to her to be careful because these guys had nothing but *Playboy* magazines in their hands that they wanted her to autograph. I encouraged her not to sign them because all they wanted was to get her autograph on her controversial, sexy photos and probably go and sell them at a high price. You could just tell some of them really weren't fans and I thought they were wrong in what they were trying to do—cash in on LaToya without really appreciating that what they have is a rare autograph from a member of one of the most famous families in the world of entertainment; the Jackson family (and treasuring it!). Upon listening to my brotherly advise, LaToya looked at me sincerely and assured me she wouldn't sign any of the *Playboy* pictorials, and she didn't. But for the loyal, and long-time fans of herself and her family, LaToya graciously signed their albums, photos, and other memorabilia, while even posing with some lucky fans who had their Polaroids ready and waiting!

The next time I saw LaToya in person was in the summer of 1993, performing in Cherry Hill, NJ. She was touring with her stage show at the time so it was my chance to see Miss Toya do her thing "live!" She was also promoting her club hit, "You're Gonna Get Rocked," which was produced by members of the Hip-Hop group, Full Force, and was making its mark on the charts. She's come a long way since her 1980 debut album entitled, *LaToya*, which featured the hit songs "If You Feel The Funk" and "Night Time Lover," a song that was written and produced by younger brother, Michael Jackson. It might have been a long time coming, but LaToya was fast becoming the celebrity as a solo artist, that didn't need to be in the shadow of her famous brothers, that she so desired.

LaToya opened her show with her brother Michael's hit song, "Wanna Be Startin' Somethin'" with two fabulous dancers enhancing her performance. The choreography was elaborate and technical, but LaToya never lost a step while she was singing and dancing. She remained in top form right up to the closing number of her show, her rendition of her brother's big hit, "Shake Your Body (Down To The Ground)." Not knowing what to expect of LaToya's performance, since it was my first time seeing her live, I was very impressed with her professionalism, her ability to hold her own on stage, her presentation, and her overall talent. It was obviously clear to see that not only does the famous Jackson talent blood run through all of the brothers, but also flows through the sisters, LaToya, Janet, and Rebbie, as well.

Janet Jackson, who is the youngest of the nine Jackson siblings, made her stage debut with her brothers, the Jackson Five, performing a series of shows in Las Vegas at the MGM Grand Hotel in 1974. Who would have known that this adorable bundle of joy would grow to have such blockbuster success in television, film, and the music industry. She not only won the hearts of millions from working with her talented family in those legendary Las Vegas shows, but also when she appeared on her first hit television show, "Good Times," 1974, and followed with other hit shows, "Diff'rent Strokes" ,1978, "A New Kind of Family," 1979, and "Fame," 1982. She was a TV darling that captivated the viewers with her charm and sunny smile, and of course, her acting abilities. But now, Janet, *Miss Jackson if you're nasty*, went on the become an international superstar and won numerous awards in the music industry for her record sales and music videos, and for her tireless efforts in support of various charity organizations. She also starred in her first feature film, *Poetic Justice*, 1993, co-starring Tupac Shakur, and directed by acclaimed director, John Singleton, who also directed brother Michael's famous video, *Remember The Time*, which featured Eddie Murphy, Magic Johnson, and supermodel, Iman. But Janet's mega success stems from her chart-topping music sales, starting with her debut album, *Janet*, in 1981, then *Control, Rhythm Nation 1814, Janet Jackson, Design Of A Decade—1986/1996*, and her most recent release, *The Velvet*

Rope. Janet Jackson has proved to herself and the world that she has total *control* of her career and she's *alright with me*.

Rebbie, the eldest of the nine Jacksons, who always remained in the shadows of her world renowned family, finally let her light shine through with the release of her debut album in 1984. It featured the hit song, "Centipede," which was written and produced by brother Michael Jackson. Her dynamic beauty, talent, and Jackson name should have earned her a higher plateau in the recording industry, but for reasons which I cannot fathom, Rebbie was overlooked by the politics of the industry, and never achieved the celebrity status she deserved. Rebbie released another album in 1988 entitled *R U Tuff Enuff*, with the single release, "Plaything." She also contributed a song "Forever Young" to the motion picture soundtrack of *Free Willy 2 (The Adventure Home)*, in 1995. Although Rebbie's career never skyrocketed into super stardom, she continues to work closely with every member of her family in their major multimedia music and film company, called Jackson Communications Inc. (JCI). She is often seen representing the Jackson family for media interviews, press conferences, etc., and remains a powerful force behind her family. Big sister Rebbie is *Yours Faithfully*, which is the title of her current album on MJJ Records, with her latest single release entitled "You Take Me Places." Looks like she's coming out of the shadows and into the light of stardom once again.

Brother Tito, the lead guitarist of the group, was scheduled to release his first solo album ever in 1990. The album entitled *Last But Not Least* would have featured a collection of some of the world's most renowned Blues artists such as B.B. King, Muddy Waters, Bo Diddley, along with other great performers. Unfortunately, this project never surfaced. The album, I'm sure, would have been a big success for Tito outside of the many hits and successes that he and the brothers have had in their careers. This would have been the first Blues album by a member of the Jackson family, displaying the range of talent and versatility of Tito Jackson.

And, "last but not least," as brother Tito would say, are the 3 sons of Tito himself: Taj, T.J., and Taryll, better known as "3T," who have displayed a multitude of talent through their singing and music. The first recording of the brothers "T" was a track for the Jackson family television mini-series, "The Jacksons: An American Dream," entitled, "You Are The Ones," which was written by 3T in honor of the Jackson brothers, their father and uncles. 3T also sang with the Jacksons on the song, "The Dream Goes On," another hit from the Jacksons' television mini-series. 3T put their foot a little further in the door and went on to record the songs "Didn't Mean To Hurt You" from the motion picture *Free Willy*, 1993, "What Will It Take" from *Free Willy 2 (The Adventure Home)*, 1995, and "Waiting For Love" from the *Men In Black* soundtrack starring Will Smith and Tommy Lee Jones, 1997. All this was just a stepping stone for their debut album, *Brotherhood*, on MJJ Productions record label, featuring the hit singles "Anything," "I Need You," "Why" and "Tease Me." Who would have imagined; a second generation of Jackson brothers! But... *the dream goes on!*

I had the pleasure of meeting 3T and their manager, Mr. Frank DiLeo, in New York City, December 16, 1995 at the annual Kwanzaa Festival held in the Jacob Javitz Convention Center. You may or may not know the man and his name, *Frank DiLeo*, but Frank DiLeo became Michael Jackson's manager during the time that *Thriller* was released, and helped mastermind the success of the world's greatest entertainer. Now he's bringing 3T to greater heights with their careers by working together closely with their father, Tito Jackson. The Kwanzaa Fest, a spiritual event for the celebration of Kwanzaa, was the perfect place for 3T to perform and meet their fans from the New York area. The yearly event generates one of the city's largest number of Black visitors, and 3T's fans came out in droves to see them! When 3T, Taj, Taryll and T.J., came on-stage to perform, it was so amazing to see how many young "teenybopper" fans were there supporting them, *screaming* for them just like the days of the Jackson Five and their "Jacksonmania!" I remember the Jacksonmania days very well and this was exactly the same kind of hysteria that the Jackson Five created back in the early 70's. After their performance they came out to sign autographs for the fans and the girls just swarmed around them like bees on honey! And before they left that day, I got the chance to meet them backstage and congratulate them on their success. They are such talented, personable young men, their smiles radiate across the room like the sun shining brightly. I am so proud of them for carrying on the Jackson tradition of great music and *brotherhood*. Their success all over the world has only just begun.

TOUCHED BY THE JACKSONS

CHAPTER 26

Dangerous

With Michael Jackson's soon-to-be-released album nearing its release date, Michael, and a few other people, had something "new" in mind. It was rumored that Madonna was the first to suggest the idea publicly as she spoke to the press one day about the possibility of her and Michael collaborating on a song together. That was in the planning stages, but more than anything she wanted to redo Michael's entire look and give him a new image. Get rid of that long hair, the buckled boots and clothing, and try something completely new, off the wall. It is also reported that Michael's manager contacted several top fashion designers to create ideas for a new Michael Jackson! Whatever the truth of the matter was, the "Fox 5 News" in New York City got wind of it and decided to do their own makeover for Michael, but they had one problem: they couldn't get Michael Jackson himself to participate! So who did they call... the next best thing to Michael himself... *Phoenix*!! Yes, on May 20, 1991, I became the model for "Fox 5 News'" Michael Jackson makeover.

"Fox 5 News" used Madonna's suggestion as their angle and hired Madonna's hair dresser, Max Pinnell, her make-up artist, Lydia Snyder, and a clothing stylist for *Esquire* magazine, Tony Melillo, as my makeover staff. We spent the early part of the day coordinating and selecting designer outfits, creating a new hair style, and changing make-up techniques. We then moved ourselves and all of our necessities to complete the transformation to another shooting location in downtown Manhattan. They first shot me looking like the old Michael Jackson, with long wavy hair and strands of it hanging in my face, black buckled boots and pants, and silver spandex stage shirt. Then it all came together as Max Pinnell got to chopping on my hair and cut it into a very short, modern style, going for a drastic change. Lydia Snyder softened the make-up Michael wore, arching the brows a bit and creating a more natural look. And Tony Melillo narrowed down his designer looks to the following choices; an Hermes vest and Chester Barrie suit, a concert look by Patricia Fields, a trendy black lycra fitted outfit by Gianni Versace, and everybody's favorite, a stylish Jean Paul Gaultier black and white striped jump suit, chosen exclusively because he's Madonna's favorite designer!

    Everyone was in motion all around me as they busily prepared for the shooting of their creative ideas and bring it all to life, and I was loving every minute of it! As the director shot me "performing" in each new outfit, I had the opportunity to express myself freely as to what I thought Michael Jackson might do if he was wearing that outfit. There were no boundaries as they allowed me my creative freedom to create whatever I felt Michael would do with each new look. Everyone at the studio treated me like royalty and I felt like the King of Pop myself! Even though it was a long day for all of us, working nonstop for 12 hours straight, the atmosphere remained friendly and upbeat until we finished; no stressed out workers by any means. And when it all came to a close, I was sorry it was over. We had so much fun doing this project that it hardly seemed like work at all. That same week, the "Fox 5 Evening News" segment, "Fox Style News" featured the Madonna inspired, Michael Jackson makeover, starring ME, and aired across the country on Fox's sister stations! Surely Mr. Jackson was bound to see it in L.A., or at least one of his personal assistants! I was very pleased with the entire project and was curious to find out Michael's thoughts and reactions to it, but never did. Deep in my mind I believe Michael saw it somehow, some way, and was impressed by his makeover.

Maybe as impressed as I was when I met Jermaine Jackson for the second time in New York, on Election Day, November 1992. He was appearing on the "Live! With Regis and Kathie Lee" show, on ABC-TV, promoting the Jacksons' upcoming television mini-series, produced by Jermaine himself, entitled "The Jacksons: An American Dream." The mini-series was a first time ever story of the Jackson family and how the magic all began with the story of Katherine and Joseph Jackson, their children, and their lives, struggling together before the days of fame and the Jackson Five, living their *American Dream* of success and stardom as the world's most famous family of entertainers. It was the opportunity of a lifetime for Jermaine to produce his first television mini-series, and for it to be the story of his own family. And with the help of Motown veteran, Suzanne dePasse, his mother Katherine, and other family members, Jermaine put his talents to the test and scored the highest marks for his production of "The Jacksons: An American Dream."

Once news hit the industry insiders that they were going to be casting in New York for various roles of the Jackson brothers for the mini-series, I was contacted by one of my agents to audition. I anxiously jumped at the opportunity to really portray Michael Jackson in a movie about his life as a famous Jackson brother; a dream come true! But as you may have noticed, I unfortunately did not get the role of Michael Jackson, but was glad I was even considered for the part. All in all, the acclaimed mini-series was a big success for Jermaine and the entire Jackson family, even if I didn't get to play Michael!

Jermaine also expanded his talents into becoming the Executive Producer of the Jackson family's very own "Jackson Family Honors" television special. Originally scheduled to be held at the Atlantic City Civic Center in Atlantic City, New Jersey, on December 11, 1993, the event was postponed and rescheduled at the MGM Grand Hotel and Casino in Las Vegas, Nevada, and aired on the NBC network, February 22, 1994. The historical event was described as one family coming together in a celebration of music, dedication, and charity, to celebrate the works of others and to help those that are less fortunate. The Jackson family extravaganza featured all the members of the Jackson family, including the grandchildren, except for sister LaToya. The Jacksons presented Lifetime Achievement Awards to two individuals who demonstrated significant contributions of unselfish dedication and sacrifice to others: Motown founder and legend, Berry Gordy, who opened the doors of Motown to numerous Black recording artists, including the Jackson Five, providing the support and promotion necessary to succeed in the music industry, creating the "Motown Legends" of today—Stevie Wonder, Marvin Gaye, The Supremes, Smokey Robinson and The Miracles, The Four Tops, The Temptations, The Marvelettes, Mary Wells, Martha and The Vandellas, Junior Walker and the All Stars, and of course, the Jackson Five ; and actress/humanitarian, Elizabeth Taylor, for her years of tireless dedication around the world to the cause, the education, and the cure of the AIDS virus. Proceeds from ticket sales were being donated to various select charities that have helped society and the less fortunate internationally, that are dedicated to children, education, shelter, and wildlife. And in celebration of music, the "Jackson Family Honors" featured performances by the entire Jackson family, special individual performances by Janet Jackson and Jermaine Jackson, and guest performances by Smokey Robinson, Gladys Knight, and Dionne Warwick. We can all learn from the noble humanitarian efforts of these celebrities and others who have tried to bring the world together and unite for a common purpose. *Just believe in the blessings of life, in the pure and the sane and the truth and the light, and the power of love... If you'd only believe.*

As Jermaine was coming out of the studio after taping the "Live! With Regis and Kathie Lee" show, I met him walking into the lobby of the ABC-TV building after the taping. All eyes were on Jermaine as he entered the lobby, looking distinguished in his navy blue pin striped suit. The women there were practically tripping over their own feet trying to get close to him for a photo or an autograph. I was feeling under the weather that day, but managed to get a photo with Jermaine despite my fever. He was very cordial with his fans, even though he seemed a bit rushed. Sometimes there just isn't enough time for small talk! And as he drove away, waving to his fans from his limousine, he was like *two ships on the ocean, waving good-bye.*

Michael Jackson's 4th release, *Dangerous*, on Sony/Epic Records, in 1992, was the most progressive of all his albums to date, with the clever arrangements, advanced technology, and distinctly creative approach, much like that of the Beatles' *Sgt. Pepper's Lonely Hearts Club Band* album. The music was a unique combination of R & B, Hip Hop, Classical, Opera, Rock, Gospel, and Soul and very un-Jackson-esque, except for perhaps a song or two. It was also the first solo album that Michael did for Sony/Epic Records without the producing efforts of Quincy Jones, which dispelled and defeated the rumors that Michael Jackson could not work without the ingenious help of Quincy.

Instead, Michael chose to work with the young, urban innovator of the "New Jack Swing" musical style, a sound that has added a new flavor to the music industry about a decade ago and has carried into the music of today. The brilliant producing talents of Teddy Riley, creator and King of the New Jack Swing, were the source behind the new sound Michael wanted to project, along with his own imaginative writing and producing talents.

"Black Or White," the first single release from the album, *Dangerous*, was undoubtedly the most Pop oriented, Jackson sounding song from the album. A typical record company choice for a first release, hoping to cash in on the loyal long-time fans of Michael, without hitting them with the artistic new music from the album first; that would be too risky financially for them. But with the release of "Black Or White" came Michael's elaborate video for the song, which premiered on MTV, BET, and the Fox Network simultaneously. What they did expect was millions of viewers around the world tuning in to the music video premiere sure to top anything Michael has done to date. What they didn't expect was the widespread controversy and disturbing reaction from the viewers.

The video in its long form, contains a closing dance sequence in which Michael Jackson "morphs" into a black panther and portrays his interpretation of the panther's animalistic behavior through dance. People everywhere were flabbergasted, appalled, disgusted if you will, by the violent and sexual display of Michael's interpretive dance of the panther. Calls and letters from angry viewers flooded the networks and forced Michael into editing the final minutes of the video containing the controversial material and issuing a statement of apology to the world. Frankly, I think the public overreacted to the contents of the video solely because it was

Michael Jackson. Had another artist done the same exact thing in their video, it never would have caused the same outrageous reaction and probably wouldn't have caused any of the media madness in the least. Some may call it a publicity stunt on Michael's behalf, creating a lot of hoopla and attention for his new single and album release. Others think it was an honest miscalculation of the public's reaction from Michael, the networks, and Sony/Epic Records. Either way, "Black Or White" was causing quite a commotion and the public wanted more.

Other singles soon followed, including, "Remember The Time," "In The Closet," "Jam," "Will You Be There," and "Heal The World," all proving to be successful for Michael and *Dangerous*. His Dangerous World Tour began in Munich, Germany and carried him throughout the world. Michael even visited his homeland, the "Motherland," Africa, for his "Come Back To Eden" tour of the land, and was overwhelmingly received by his African brothers and sisters. His people were so honored to have Michael, the most successful entertainer in the entire world, representative of them as a Black African man, that he was in turn honored with nobility as an honorary "King of Sani," and with the admirable Medal of Honor from the President of Gabon. While touring through different African countries, Michael devoted a generous amount of time to visiting children in hospitals, orphanages, schools, churches, and institutions, and enjoyed their culture and traditions with them. As Michael completed his spiritual uplifting trip to the land of his roots, he continued to play to record breaking capacities around the world. His Dangerous Tour, which began in June 1992, lasted over a year, spanning the globe, country to country, until the Fall of 1993. But before Michael returned to the U.S. for the tail end of his tour in America, a bomb was dropped.

CHAPTER 27
The Nightmare

Michael Jackson, the King of Pop, philanthropist, lover of all animals, and especially fond of children, was being accused of alleged child molestation charges. The headlines were everywhere you looked, all over the world, obviously taking precedence over more important matters of the day, that took a backseat to the media circus. Michael Jackson was being charged with molesting a 13 year old boy, whom he had befriended, and the newspapers, magazines, tabloid papers and TV shows, plastered the disturbing allegations on every issue, edition, or broadcast that they could. This, I believe, was nothing but a sheer case of extortion, carried out by the boy's father, the mastermind behind the master plan, who coerced his own son into making the allegations. The boy's father tried to manipulate the media into brainwashing the public into believing that Michael Jackson, the man who has given so much love, compassion, and financial support, to children all around the world, trying to *heal the world*, was guilty of such hideous accusations. In my opinion, it seems to me that the boy's father wanted to dethrone the King himself, and tried his best to get the public on his side and believe him and his son. It's a shame that so many people actually fell into the man's scheme of extortion and believed that Michael was guilty. The media, as usual, turned all the ugly rumors into a circus and all you saw or heard anywhere, anytime, anyplace, was the child molestation charges against Michael. But the more they talked about it, the more I knew deep down in my heart that he was innocent. And so did the Jackson family.

Michael's family and close friends came forward to defend his innocence... all except for sister LaToya. Once again, LaToya was a rebel without a cause talking negatively to the press about her family, specifically, brother Michael. It's an embarrassment that LaToya had to come out in such a way to the public that one can only conclude that her only interest is money. It was obvious she was talking to tabloid shows and news programs for large sums of money, but talk is cheap, and so is selling yourself and your family to the public. LaToya is a source, a powerful source to the media because she is a Jackson, and as a Jackson, she would assumably have the most reliable information about her famed family. But what LaToya didn't seem to realize is that since she and her family are one of the most highly recognized, most highly publicized families in the world, anything you say or do can be held against you. And when LaToya sowed her words against Michael and other members of her family, the Jackson family came to Michael's defense viciously to un-reap what LaToya and the press had sowed.

When the Jackson family came forth in support of Michael, they were like championship boxers entering the ring for Round 1 of the grudge match fight against their greatest opponent, the press, and were determined to knock them out. In all the years I've seen the Jacksons at press conferences, interviews, etc., never, ever have I seen them so emotionally charged with rage and anger than I did when they spoke out for Michael in defense of his innocence. Even mother, Katherine Jackson, obviously infuriated with the whole scenario, had fire in her eyes and spoke audaciously to the press when interviewed, for the first time ever. The Jacksons were angry at the molestation charges against Michael, the press for magnifying and sensationalizing the situation, and LaToya for betraying Michael and the family's loyalty. Michael had enough *bad* press being printed and reported every day across the globe, he didn't need his own sister adding fuel to the fire that was slowly burning him.

Brother Jermaine said that Michael was made a victim of a cruel and obvious attempt to take advantage of his fame. Brother Tito stated that it was a setup and Michael would win this hands down. The members of the Jackson family that did speak to the press were very upset with people close to Michael that they felt were getting paid to turn on him and speak against him. There is a saying in the Bible that sister Rebbie quoted, "Do not put your trust in nobles nor in the son of earthly man," a powerful statement that perhaps Michael should have taken heed to. Perhaps he trusted those people closest to him, and they were the ones that turned against him, but not until the allegations were made public. Seems to me if they had any complaints about Michael and his conduct or misconduct, then they should have aired them at the appropriate time and place. Not jump on the bandwagon of former Michael employees trying to cash in on their story for a quick buck. And you know as well as I do, the tabloid papers and TV shows feasted on the juicy information like leeches on an open wound and the public fervently ate it up, like *tabloid junkies*. Remember, in the words of Michael Jackson, *just 'cause you read it in a magazine or see it on a TV screen, don't mean it's factual, or actual. And you don't have to read it, and you don't have to eat it, to buy it is to feed it...* In other words, don't be a *tabloid junkie*!!

But even before this ordeal hit the tabloids, another story surfaced from within the Jackson family. In 1992, Jermaine Jackson wrote a song, "Word To The Badd," which was a verbal lash out at his brother Michael. According to Jermaine, the song was supposed to never have been released commercially, but somehow, someway, that song found its way from one top radio station to another, all across the country, and in no time, flooded the airways. Jermaine was basically upset with Michael because he couldn't get next to his own brother or even have any of his calls returned. Jermaine is Michael's family, his blood, and he felt like was being treated like *a stranger in Moscow*. At first Jermaine thought that maybe Michael was getting a little too big, a little too far and removed from reality, and losing touch with himself and the world. Jermaine wanted to express his anger and hurt, hoping his brother would reach out to him. But since his gripe with his brother became like dirty laundry hanging on the line for the press, they soaked it, rinsed through it, and wrung out every ounce of "juice" they could from it, causing more grief than the words of the song ever could have. They turned it into the Battle of the Brothers, Jackson vs. Jackson. It didn't take too long for the whole situation to get ugly, because once the press gets the scoop, a rumor, or even an inkling about something, it is broadcasted all over the world, especially if your last name is *Jackson*.

    Once Jermaine had just about enough of the media morons, he came out attacking the press capitalizing on his family once again. He was angry that his message was misinterpreted and blown out of proportion. Jermaine stated in several interviews that his song was "creative anger," and he was expressing his anger the best way he knows how—through music. But, most importantly, the song was a *healing*, a chance for Michael to realize Jermaine's and other family members feelings, and rectify the problem. Jermaine said that Michael has too many "Yes" people working for him, and people like that are too busy trying to kiss ass to keep their job, like everything Michael says or does is a "Yes Mr. Jackson," but they're not really doing their job in the best interest of Michael. If Michael tells them he's not receiving any calls today, and his mother Katherine calls, even expresses the importance of her call, well sorry, but Mr. Jackson is unavailable today. If Michael is on tour and staying in a hotel somewhere and Michael tells his people not to let anyone in to see him, and brother Jermaine just happens to be traveling in the same place at the same time and tries to go visit brother Michael, well sorry, but no one is allowed to see Michael. Yes sir, that means NO ONE!! This is what Jermaine was so pissed off with that he just had to let his brother know! Maybe Michael wasn't even getting their messages at all for all he knew! But once Michael did get the message, he heard it loud and clear and reconciled with his brother and family immediately. The song certainly was a healing song because *it all begins and ends with love.*

But I can truly understand Jermaine's feelings about his brother, Michael Jackson, because at one point, I had the same feelings about him myself. I felt Michael was losing touch with himself and his people, the Black people, and I, too, expressed my anger creatively, in a short story I wrote entitled, "Michael Jackson: Who Are You" in 1991. There were things about Michael that I questioned, didn't understand, or just could not accept about Michael and through my story I expressed my thoughts. I eagerly sent my manuscript to several entertainment publications in hopes that my story would be read by Michael. I wanted to be heard and for Michael to hear me. Although, the several publications were interested and wanted to use my story, I decided to withdraw my manuscript because it was already heard... by Michael. My story must have sparked a fire somewhere and the flames spread to Michael because I got numerous phone calls from one of Michael's attorneys. He conveyed Michael's concerns of my story and wanted to offer me some valuable insight on Michael Jackson; the celebrity and the man. Michael's attorney confided in me the many charitable organizations and cultural projects that Mr. Jackson is involved in and has contributed to generously that were not publicized. Michael is very concerned with his public image, particularly to his loyal fans, and did not want to be misrepresented in any way by my story. But yet he is only human, just the same as you and me, and has the right to do whatever he wishes with his time, money, and his heart. I've learned that there's a lot more to Michael Jackson, the humanitarian, and the man, than meets the eye, and he has proven me wrong in so many ways since then.

I declined having my story published because I didn't want to shed any negative light on Michael or myself as a loyal fan. And I truly feel that maybe my story enlightened Michael in such a way where he felt a need to share even more his involvement and contributions to numerous organizations with the public so we could feel even closer to him as a human being. And his own self created Heal The World Foundation, which was designed to help contribute to many worthy charities such as the Minority AIDS Foundation, Make A Wish Foundation, Camp Ronald McDonald, and Pediatric AIDS, just to name a few, was one of the most obvious displays of Michael's sincere love and affection for children, his Black people, and all of mankind. I'm just thrilled to proclaim that I've come to a much higher understanding and respect of Michael and know in my heart who Michael Jackson *really is!*

That's why I just can't let myself believe the trash and allegations against Michael. This man who is the biggest and most successful entertainer, uh Black entertainer, in *history*, who has broken records worldwide in record sales and concert attendance, who has broken down more doors and paved an even larger path for other Black performers, who has given immeasurable amounts of time and money to charities and organizations, who has demonstrated his love for children, all children of the world, how could you believe he was guilty? Since the media was acting as the courtroom in his case, Michael was being tried publicly, and through the eyes of the "system," he was perceived as being guilty. They wanted the public to convict him first, before he was legally tried, as they corruptly carried out their so-called investigation through every news medium possible. Talk about brainwashing... With all the wealth, fame, power, and success that Michael Jackson has achieved in his career, it seems to me that they wanted nothing more than to convict him and knock the reigning King of Pop off his throne. In other words, knock the powerful Black man out of power. Once upon a time, you were "innocent until proven guilty," but now it seems you are guilty until proven innocent, if you're Black, that is. Oh yes, "the truth shall set you free," unless you're a Black man in America. I speak not of thoughts and opinions, but of knowledge and experience. Knowledge that there have been many a Black personality, professional athlete, political figure, and entertainer that has been treated with the same disrespect and corruption as Mr. Jackson by the press, and more importantly, by the "system." Experience that I, too, have been treated with the same injustice and corruption as some of the world's most famous, most renowned Black men. Experience that I, too, was a victim of the system.

TOUCHED BY THE JACKSONS

CHAPTER 28
Why You Wanna Trip On Me

My nightmare began after the birth of my daughter... after her mother heard for the umpteenth time that I was not going to make a life with her... after her mother realized I was not going to be a part of the furniture in her household... after she could no longer deal with the situation because she couldn't have everything she wanted. She wanted Me, and just couldn't have Me; she could only have Me as Timanda's Father, and well, that just wasn't enough for her. She wanted the storybook romance, the house with the white picket fence around it, and me to share it with, but *how can you build a castle of sand, when we know very well it will never stand*? I was not her knight in shining armor. I did not come and save her, the pitiful damsel in distress, from her own misery and self imposed agony. She was obsessed and possessed, and could not control her actions or her emotions. She is the type of person that once scorned, will never get over it, and seeks vengeance upon those that hurt her, never once thinking of the consequences that she may face. All she thinks about is revenge, and seeks it with the most evil, most sinister way she can imagine, never once thinking of herself or our daughter first.

When she first found out she was pregnant, she jumped out of the frying pan and into the fire because I would not move in with her. So in spite of me, she cut off her nose to spite her face, and wound up living in a woman's shelter because she just left her apartment and wanted me to come and rescue her, to prove to her that I cared. Well, of course I cared, she was pregnant with our daughter and I didn't want to see her living in some shelter with strangers, so I ran around like a lunatic trying to get her out of the shelter and into a new place by the time our daughter was born. And I did, thank God, but that was only the beginning of my nightmare.

Each day was like another scene of my eternal nightmare as I tried to live happily and enjoy the special time spent with my daughter, but this woman wreaked so much havoc upon me that I felt like I was never going to awake from this frightening dream. Never a day went by that this woman did not try to kill my spirit, verbally abuse me, or try to manipulate me, all the while using my daughter as her shield, knowing how much love I have for my child. And because I do love my daughter that much, I went along with mostly everything she asked or needed of me, for the sake of my daughter. I helped her get that apartment so she would have a nice place to call home for her and my daughter. God knows, I was there when most guys wouldn't be; I was there as Timanda's father for whatever she needed, and even went the extra mile for her mother for anything she needed as well—a new winter coat, new shoes, whatever. I would have even given her my last if she needed it because that's the type of person I am. I was even the one to petition her into court for visitation and child support of my daughter; most men don't volunteer to financially support their kids unless the mother forces them into court, but I took on the responsibility willingly. As noble a gesture that it was, she never appreciated it. It was never enough for her, never, because she didn't have me. She wanted to see me hurt because she hurt, she wanted me to feel miserable because she was miserable, she wanted me to *scream* and argue because she constantly liked to *scream* and argue, she wanted to bring me down because she was down, she wanted me to be discouraged because she felt discouraged... in other words, I could not be *happy* when I spoke to her, or was standing in her presence because she wanted to rain on my parade. Hey, I can't help it if the sun shines in my life everyday!

As time went on, my child's mother became more and more out of control and had to find another way to avenge me—through the courts. She had me arrested twice on bogus charges, which the judge quickly dismissed because they were unfounded. It was a desperate attempt to stop my visitations, **again**, knowing how much love I have for my child, she figured if she stops my visitations with the child, I'll fight 'til the end of time for her and take whatever blows she throws at me because of my daughter. Well that's very true, but I fought back like Tyson in the ring, trying to get that knockout before the end of the round, because I was fighting for my child. Believe me, I was not about throw a fight and go down with nothing. But at least I was fighting fair; she, on the other hand, was hitting below the belt in court and lying and manipulating them into believing her ridiculous stories and accusations. But the joke of it was, everything she said about me they took as the truth and never questioned it or investigated her claims whatsoever. It was then that I learned what the word CORRUPTION meant. It was then that I realized I couldn't win because there was cheating going on. Once you see that nobody's playing the game fairly, you have to get out before you get fucked over. But like a fool, I stayed in the game longer for the sake of my daughter, but all I accomplished was financial gain for my lawyers and the court system. The so-called "family" court system doesn't care about me, my daughter, or her mother... they only care about one thing—generating funds;

they really don't care about us. If the court system truly operated in the proper manner, "in the best interest of the child," then you wouldn't have so many families torn apart or children suffering. But they don't work in that manner, and that's why my daughter's mother had custody of our daughter even though she had a *history* of going in and out of numerous shelters since that first one when she was pregnant because <u>**she**</u> chose to put herself in that environment. You tell me that my daughter living with her mother is in the best interest of the child.... *right*. But I was living in a nice home with my wife, in a safe environment, with a decent income between the two of us, and I was the "bad guy" that couldn't have custody of his daughter. Sure, have my daughter live with her mother, whom in my opinion, at the time, was unstable, mentally incompetent, emotionally imbalanced, who has been from shelter to shelter, trying to break the bond between the child and her father... yes, by all means, that would be the most logical thing to do "in the best interest of the child." ***Right***. Oh, I understand the rules now... keep the child away from the father for as long as possible because he's paying for his attorney and he's fighting back in court with every dollar and every piece of ammunition he's got, and he's gonna continue fighting until he gets what he wants. Wow, do you know how long that's going to take and how much money he's going to have to spend to do that?! Thousands and thousands of dollars! *Bleed him!!* This so-called system which should be designed to keep families together has systematically and methodically torn families apart, especially those that are interracial, multi cultural, or "different" in their eyes. They are not acting in the best interest of the child or in the best interest of the family. Believe me, they cut me deep and tried to bleed me to death, but she still didn't stop. She had to take it to the extreme, to the next level, because she still was not satisfied. She had to come up with something so powerful, that the court would believe her, even without any physical evidence, and cut off my rights as a father.

I, like Michael Jackson, was charged with a crime I didn't commit. The mother of my daughter accused me of Custodial Interference in the 1st degree, which quite simply means interfering with the custody of my child. Hmm... interfering with custody... sounds pretty harmless and minor, and in truth, actually is, but in that racist county court in which this charge was brought against me, it must mean kidnapping, armed robbery, and attempted murder! Sounds ridiculous... perhaps, but this ridiculous and petty accusation was to that county what the Michael Jackson case was to the Los Angeles county court. I was the local celebrity that I feel they wanted to dethrone and extort money from, the only difference was that the accusation against me was a minor offense by great comparison to the charges against Michael Jackson. In my opinion, this racist court took the case to a level far beyond the realm of the circumstances and tried to fuck me over like my last name was "Jackson." The only lame, bogus excuse they had is that my daughter was found in my custody, which by coincidence, was during the time of my legal visitation with her. When we were brought to the precinct, I could see the look of fear in her eyes that this was far too much for her to handle. I did not want my daughter to see me in this situation, even though I did nothing wrong. She was just 3 years old at the time and didn't understand what was going on and why she couldn't be with her Daddy there. When it was time for me to leave because they had to transfer me to another holding facility, I asked the officer not to let my daughter see me that way, with handcuffs on. He covered them up with my jacket so Timanda would not see them and be scared. She came running towards me crying hysterically, and broke through the wall of policemen around me. She jumped into my arms, and held onto me so tightly that I could feel every ounce of strength in her body, and she wouldn't let go. It was as if she knew she wasn't going to see me for a while. I told her not to worry because Daddy will see her again real soon, but I could tell by the look on her face that she didn't quite believe me. She knew this was not right and was too young to fully express her feelings, but her face told me all that she wanted to say. That was a day that I knew my daughter had become emotionally scarred by what her mother had done.

First, I was indicted by a grand jury, in a so-called secret indictment, for Custodial Interference in the 1st degree, a crime that is considered an E-felony in that county court, and held without bail until my arraignment before the Superior Court. When I went before the Superior Court a few days later, the judge did impose bail for me... only *$150,000*!! My bail was ***$150,000***! A bail of that caliber would be considered a "ransom bail" in most courts. And is some cases, even murderers don't get bails that high! This outrageous bail was set not because of the so-called crime I was allegedly accused of, but for three reasons: 1. I was a Black man. 2. I was a successful Black man. 3. I had a child by a White woman. And the judge, whom I feel was racist, senile, and an ignorant fool, fed into the D.A.'s accusations, which were nothing but a wing and a prayer, trying to keep yet another Black man behind bars. And I remained behind bars for almost three months, for a crime I did not commit. This 3-ring circus court was led by the ringleader, the D.A., and all the other people participating were the clowns. It just amazes me that the D.A. in this case, flat out lied about me in so many statements, probably hoping that the case wouldn't have to go to trial because the evidence would have to support the outlandish allegations. The judge took his prejudices and the D.A.'s accusations and turned it into the most evil game of hangman called "Hang the Nigga." Let me give you my definition of the term D.A.: the term D.A. may technically stand for District Attorney, but in my opinion, this D.A. stands for "Devil's Advocate." As D.A.'s, some use the forces of evil to carry out their work as *perpetrators*, to come through with convictions and guilty verdicts on people who maybe really are guilty, but also for the people that are innocent and don't deserve it. It seems to me that everybody gets fucked over by the D.A.'s like that Michael Jackson song "DS," it should have been titled "**DA!**" I know and God knows that I am guilty of nothing, except loving my daughter. But I decided to throw in the towel into pleading guilty to a crime I did not commit. I pleaded guilty not because I was guilty, but because I knew that my daughter's happiness and sanity are the most important issues in this matter, as well as my entire family's sanity. I was not about to keep fighting with a person that cares about no one but herself or whose lives she's affecting. I could not let my daughter continue to see the madness that her mother was creating and have it pose a negative influence on her. I literally had to stop fighting before things got too carried away. I had to for my daughter's sake, for my sons' sake, for my wife's sake, for my sake, and for all my family and friends that love me. I had to put my daughter in God's hands by putting her feelings first, knowing that He would make a way out of no way. And I can truly understand and sympathize with Michael Jackson for also being forced into a settlement. Because of his name, his wealth, and his reputation as the world's biggest superstar, his case could have been in litigation for several years, and could have had very damaging effects on his career. It would have been very detrimental to his image as a celebrity, a humanitarian, and a human being having these harmful allegations associated with his name and status being dragged all throughout the media. Michael was forced into a settlement for an undisclosed amount of money because it was the only way he could keep his sanity and his life. But for those that may think that by Michael settling out of court, it is an admission of his guilt, are very disillusioned by the media and reality. It is not "buying your way out"; it is paying the extortion money so you can possibly have your life back and live peacefully once again. Believe me, no one knows that better than myself because I am living proof of that. I am a very proud Black man, a very proud father, and have been denied the rights to see my daughter due to the mother's lies and deceptions that were injected into an already infected, biased court. Even the local daily newspaper had the balls to print such filth and garbage about me, when there's so many more important or interesting things going on in this world, *why you wanna trip on me* and print all the trash from the local courts. *Black man, black mail, throw the brother in jail. Beat me, hate me, you could never break me. Will me, thrill me, you could never kill me. Jew me, sue me, everybody do me. Kick me, Kike me, don't you Black or White me. All I wanna say is they don't really care about us.*

Throughout my daughter's existence on this earth, I have been the best nurturing, loving father that a good, caring father can be. I have never ever turned my back on my daughter. But my daughter's mother lied and manipulated the courts into believing her allegations and knowingly, because she herself is a White woman, used a racially biased system against me. But how could she do something so wicked as to use that racist system against me, knowing that the child she carried in her for nine months is Black, just like her father. And if she had any knowledge of the struggle of the Black race, fighting so hard for so many years for equality, justice, and equal rights, then she wouldn't have put her daughter's father through these channels. But since she used her words like a sword against me, the Superior Court Criminal judge imposed a ridiculous five year Order of Protection, prohibiting me from any form of contact with my daughter for five years, along with a five year probation, as part of his sentencing. How could he make that kind of determination without any type of evidence to support his decision? *I'm tired of being a victim of shame. You're throwing me in a class with a bad name. I can't believe this is the land in which I came.* The judge was playing the Devil's Advocate by abolishing any and all contact with my daughter for the next five years, certainly NOT acting in my daughter's best interest. They broke up my family, but they will never break the chain. And my daughter's mother is largely to blame for it because she put her feelings first before our daughter's feelings and did not think about Timanda. The child's feelings are the most important, despite whatever happened between the parents, the child's feelings come first, but her mother is too selfish to see it that way because if that were not true, she wouldn't have let over three years go by without letting me see my daughter, no matter what the courts ordered. There are no winners in this situation, only losers, and the one that lost the most was my daughter, Timanda, because what the judge ordered not only hurt Timanda mentally and emotionally, but also financially. It takes a lot more than just love and affection to raise a child in today's society, it also takes money, a lot of money from both parental sources, in order to satisfy a child's needs and wants. And when that momentous time comes for me and my daughter to reunite once again, it will be like we were never apart for one second, and she will have more than she could ever want or need in this world.

My parents separated when I was young, and despite whatever differences my mother and father had, my mother never kept us from our father, under any circumstances. She may have been very angry that he had an affair, but she never tried to take him to court for adultery, divorce, alimony, child support, or even any made up allegations, just to spite him or hurt him. And she never ever tried to turn us or a court of law against our father, no matter how she felt about him. We were raised to understand and know that both parents, although living separately, are equally as important and equally responsible for raising us, and no matter what, we are first and foremost a family. My daughter's mother may have treated me like *a stranger in Moscow*, but *this time around, I ain't taking no shit*. With all the sh*t that she put me through, it made me want to *scream*, but as God would have it, I found my salvation in jail, and was reincarnated into a new "life."

My time spent incarcerated was not the punishment as "they" had anticipated; instead it was a spiritual revelation for which I am grateful for. Of course, the experience of going to jail was something I had never imagined in my wildest dreams or nightmares, but I was not about to let that racist court get any ransom money whatsoever. Even though my family and friends pulled together for me to raise over $20,000 for my bail, I wouldn't give that place the satisfaction of successfully extorting money from me. But I cried knowing how much my family and friends did for me, realizing how much love and support they gave me.

"Jail" was a side of life I never ever thought I would experience because of the lifestyle I upheld for myself and my children. But the worst part of being in jail was the fact that I was considered a criminal by the system, and I had proof of my innocence that they failed to recognize. I've always been a law abiding citizen, living clean and drug free, never any trouble or brushes with the law, as they say, in my life. But the reality of the situation gave me a whole new perspective and knowledge of the system and the disgustingly ignorant manner in which my people are treated every day, people who were either victimized by the system, or fell victim to the system, whether they were innocent or guilty, because I, too, was treated with the same disrespectful demeanor. It didn't matter; to them we were all one of the same.

As I sat and meditated day by day, thinking about my life, my existence, my children, I came to a deeper level of spiritualism within myself. Even though I was apart from my family and children, I never felt alone. I had my brothers, and I mean all brothers, Black, Hispanic, Asian, White, etc. with me, and God by my side. I tried to live the same way I had outside of that place, working out in the gym, keeping my mind and body focused, praying, meditating, and keeping my spirits lifted, for I was not about to let this take me down in any way. I was too strong mentally, physically, and spiritually to ever let that happen. And as I spent time with my brothers every day, we all achieved a higher level of wisdom and knowledge from one another. It was an education in life that the richest man couldn't buy. And every night before "lock down," when everyone gets locked into their cell for the night, me and a group of my closest brothers would get together and have our prayer meetings together. Everyone would gather around my cell as I would lead them all in prayer and meditation, praying for ourselves and one another, and giving my daily sermon as the elected "Reverend." I remained so positive and spiritual throughout my ordeal that I wanted my spirit and faith to help those brothers that felt they didn't have a prayer for themselves or anyone with faith in them. With our daily affirmations and prayers, I felt like I touched the soul of my brothers and gave them faith and a deeper relationship with the almighty God. When the time came for someone to finally go home, because even one day is too long, it sometimes hurt because it wasn't you going home. Of course, it is nothing more than the envy of their freedom, but you quickly overcome that feeling because that person is so *happy* to walk free once again, and you can only rejoice in their happiness knowing that your day will come and you'll be free, just like them, once again. Just to see someone be given back their freedom is so beautiful, it's like watching a bird soaring through the air, or a child being born and given life. And when my time came to be free, I felt like the Phoenix bird rising from the ashes, with my life renewed once again. It was a *rebirth*.

CHAPTER 29
The Rebirth

As I ascended into the light of rejuvenation, my spirit lifted me higher than I ever thought possible. I was flying so high, I felt as though I was soaring through the heavens with God. All of my prayers and affirmations that had given me strength, faith, and power, were now being revealed to me. God has blessed me and flourished me lavishly, so much that my cup hath runeth over. But when I say "lavishly" I don't necessarily mean only monetarily, I mean an abundance of the truly beautiful things in life. God has opened up so many doors for me, and presented me with so many golden opportunities, I sometimes don't know which one to grasp a hold of first! He has introduced so many new things to me: new challenges, new talents, new places, new friends... that my life has been revived, and I am rising above the clouds! I have found my true inner self and tranquillity because I am at peace with myself and I am at one with myself. In my new journey, I have been blessed with the opportunity to meet and work with so many wonderful people and famous celebrities, that I know in my heart that it is God's will. It is His divine work to give me life anew and a chance to enhance my creativity, my work, and my life by meeting the right, positive people who are equally as dedicated and spiritual about themselves.

Michael Jackson was experiencing his own rebirth... with the release of *HIStory Past, Present and Future Book I* in 1995. This double musical collection contained two separate chapters in his book of life; the first containing 15 of Michael's greatest hits from all of his previous albums, *Off The Wall, Thriller, Bad* and *Dangerous*, entitled *HIStory Begins*, and the second chapter which includes 15 powerful new songs as *HIStory Continues*. This album was a new beginning for Michael because it was an emotional display of his feelings about his life, his career, and his world. Michael dared to bare his soul to the world through his music... and he did it with the guts and fury of an Olympic champion. Each song tells a chapter in Michael's life and the entire collection of songs completes "HIStory." The new song titles alone clearly indicate Michael's newfound expression of retaliation... "They Don't Care About Us," "You Are Not Alone," "Stranger In Moscow," "Money," "This Time Around," "Childhood (Theme from "Free Willy 2")," and his duet with sister Janet Jackson, "Scream." Michael had a lot to say after his devastating battle with the press and wanted to whole world to hear *"his story."* I admire him for his courage to lash out and slap those in the face that wanted to bring him down, and couldn't. *HIStory* represents Michael's *destiny*, from the past, present, and into the future, and it's obvious to see, *HIStory Continues...*

... to the next chapter, with *Blood On The Dance Floor: HIStory In The Mix*, Michael's latest release from 1997. This musical collection contains 5 new songs, including the title cut, "Blood On The Dance Floor," along with 8 remixes of previous hits from *HIStory Past, Present & Future Book 1*.

A rebirth came for the Jackson Five as they were honored as inductees into the prestigious *Rock And Roll Hall Of Fame* in 1997. The celebrated extravaganza honored the Jackson Five's outstanding careers and their distinctive mark they've made in the *history* of music. The Jackson Five's success as the world's most famous "kid" group, remains unsurpassed in fame, record sales, and longevity throughout their careers. No other kid group compares or comes remotely close to the fame of the Jackson Five, now known as The Jacksons since their departure from Motown in 1976. In honor of their success, Diana Ross, who first introduced the Jackson Five to the world, presented the award of induction to the famed Jackson brothers; Jackie, Tito, Jermaine, Marlon, and Michael. What better way to celebrate this once in a lifetime magical event than with the same person who helped launch their careers by presenting them to the world on behalf of Motown Records... Miss Diana Ross. In giving thanks, the Jackson brothers gave special honor and recognition to the man who was responsible for their illustrious careers at Motown, the wonderful wizard of Motown himself, Mr. Berry Gordy... B-E-R-R-Y-G-O-R-D-Y! The thrill of seeing all the original members of the Jackson Five on stage together, with Berry Gordy and Diana Ross, brought tears of joy to my eyes, reminiscing about the golden days of Motown.

Motown also gave re-birth to the Jackson Five with the release of the first ever, box set collection of music by the Jackson Five entitled *Soulsation*, in 1995. This 82 track, four CD/cassette box set featured all the previous Motown hits by the group, plus those by Michael, Jermaine, and Jackie Jackson as well. This collection of music from the Jackson Five's tenure with Motown Records, 1969-1976, is by far the most complete catalog of the Jackson Five's music that Motown ever put together. One disc alone in the collection features nothing but rare and unreleased tracks from Motown's music library vaults. It is definitely a Jackson Five fan's dream with over four and a half hours of continuous Jackson Five music for your listening pleasure. The honor of having their music put into the first ever, collectible box set is a rebirth for the Jackson Five and their success with Motown Records.

The legendary Motown Records experienced its own rebirth in celebration of their 40th anniversary in 1998. This legacy of music, created and orchestrated by its founder, Berry Gordy, was built upon a dream that became a reality, and ultimately, became an empire. This shrine of music was like a garden in which the seeds of a great song were planted by the talented songwriters, fertilized by the musicians and producers, and blossomed into hits by the soulful sounds of the recording artists. Motown has created the most phenomenal amount of hit records by all their artists combined that no other record company in the world has ever generated beyond comparison. The Motown empire consists of some of the world's most famous recording artists, such as The Four Tops, Marvin Gaye, The Supremes, The Miracles, Mary Wells, The Temptations, Stevie Wonder, Martha Reeves and the Vandellas, The Marvelettes, and The Jackson Five. And as time went on, the legacy continued with the "new" artists of Motown, such as The Commodores, Rick James, DeBarge, Boyz II Men, and Queen Latifah. Celebrating 40 years of music *history*, "Hitsville USA" not only changed the course of music *history* with its famous "Motown Sound," it became a pioneer in the record industry that opened the doors and paved the way for many of today's Black artists. There is only one and will never be another Motown Records. Fifteen years ago, it was Motown's 25th anniversary... *yesterday, today, forever*. Today, the legacy of Motown continues, in its music and in our souls. After 40 years of making music, listened to and loved around the world, it's clear to see that for Motown 40... *the music is forever*.

God has continued to bless me by bringing so many wonderful, spiritual people into my life. William "Smokey" Robinson has been very much a part of my life since I was a

THE REBIRTH

child, much like the Jacksons, as the magical music of Motown that he was largely responsible for creatively, filled my house. Smokey Robinson, one of the original creative forces of Motown Records, along with its founder and president, Berry Gordy, has given the world an era of music clearly defined in music *history*, known appropriately as "The Motown Sound." His musical contributions to writing so many hit songs for many of Motown's greatest artists such as The Temptations, Martha and the Vandellas, Marvin Gaye, the Supremes, his own group, Smokey Robinson and the Miracles, and the countless artists over the last 4 decades that remade many of Motown songs that Smokey wrote, demonstrate the wealth of talent that only Smokey has been blessed with. Even the world famous Jackson Five have recorded many of Smokey's songs, turning them into their own hits, including, "Who's Loving You," "The Love I Saw In You Was Just a Mirage," "Come Around Here (I'm The One You Need)," and Michael Jackson himself recorded "You've Really Got A Hold On Me." Smokey has accomplished so much for the evolution of Black music, and has paved the way for so many Black artists and songwriters. He has written literally hundreds of songs for the numerous artists of Motown that whenever you pick up one of those records and look at the label, you'll see Smokey's name as the songwriter over and over again. Smokey has written the songs for so many Motown artists that have become hits throughout the years, that these songs had love long before they had words. The music was born through his soul, as his lyrics gave all these songs first life. So when the opportunity to meet the one and only Smokey Robinson fell into my lap (from the heavens), I was more than thrilled to meet the legendary artist that helped influence the *history* of music.

    My wife, Kristine, and I met Smokey personally when

he was performing at the Trump Plaza Hotel and Casino in Atlantic City, New Jersey on August 17, 1995. I have always been a fan and admirer of Smokey's, even more so since I first saw him perform live at the Budweiser Superfest concert at Madison Square Garden in New York City, September 11, 1982. There I remember really discovering the charismatic stage presence and superbly smooth vocal technique that Smokey possessed as he serenaded all the female fans swooning in the audience over him. I was so impressed with his live singing performance that I often included a selection of his songs in my rehearsals just to keep my voice primed to singing in Smokey's unique melodic tone. It was too long since I had seen Smokey perform "live," and I was ready to see the "King of Love Songs" take the stage once again.

I always knew how great Smokey was live, but never could I have imagined the soulful expression, the mastered technique of Smokey's melodic voice as he sang from the very depths of his heart and soul. He improved upon perfection, like a fine wine aged for years, as his golden voice carried throughout the arena like the voice of an angel. Smokey was always the effervescent performer that poured his love and emotions into his work, and used his vocals like an instrument, hitting each and every note effortlessly. And after his awesome performance, we were invited backstage by Smokey's drummer, Tony Lewis, to meet the man himself. We first spoke with Smokey's Tour Director and Chief of Security, Earl Bryant, who greeted us warmly like we were old friends for years. We conversed with him for a few minutes until Smokey had a free moment, and then he introduced us to Smokey, the friendliest and sincerest gentleman I ever met. Smokey is a rare gem, with so much warmth, sincerity, and a heart of gold, you are instantly welcomed into his heart. I have to say though that in all my years, never have I met someone like Smokey who is so genuinely humble and so full of love and life, he opened his arms and heart to us, and accepted us as family. He is such an extraordinary human being, you almost see him as being bigger than life itself. And after seeing him perform live so many times, it's amazing to witness the raw talent that flows from within him; it is obvious that he is one of the few "chosen" ones in this world. His strong presence and spirit fill the room and you are instantly drawn to him and the "glow" that surrounds him because he is a child of God. As a child of God myself, I instantly felt a spiritual connection to him and my *destiny* to meet the man whom I would call my friend and brother. And from that day on, he has remained a true, loyal friend of mine whom I cherish and our bond of brotherhood will never break. Even the people that work with Smokey are equally as wonderful and personable, such as his drummer and friend, Tony Lewis and his Tour Director and Chief of Security, Earl Bryant.

Earl Bryant and I developed a close friendship, as well as a business relationship, almost instantaneously. I respect and admire him for the wonderful person that he is, and his professionalism and business expertise which comes from his years of experience working in the entertainment industry. I've learned so much more about the industry just by speaking with him and working closely with him. He has taught me so much and has shown me more about the real inside of the entertainment industry that he has strongly influenced my own personal business practices and my life. Outside of our business relationship, we've also formed a close bond of friendship that will always remain. And learning from such a great man, I know I will continue to prosper.

Tony Lewis, a talented young musician, whose resume

of entertainment includes formerly working with great artists such as Lou Rawls, George Benson, the mighty Jacksons, and many others, established an instant rapport with me. He shared with me so many wonderful stories of working with the world famous Jacksons as a drummer during their 1978-1979 Destiny Tour, and knowing them personally. The Jacksons are such a close knit family and the *brotherhood* between them is extraordinary; working side by side with them was like working with family. They are a great bunch of guys that made the grueling time on the road so much fun for everyone, it was hardly like "work" at all. Tony extended his hands of kindness to me and my wife at the first Atlantic City show that we saw Smokey and his band perform, and since then, has built a lasting friendship with me for which I am thankful for. Again, God has brought another wonderful, spiritual person to me, like it was *destiny*. Tony is like a brother to me and having worked with the Jacksons, just like Smokey in the Jackson Five's early days, is another connection to my *destiny* and *history*. But I have faith in knowing that *destiny* will keep Earl, Tony and Smokey in my life as I continue to walk down new paths with God's blessings.

Also, I was honored with a meeting *via* telephone call from another famous former Motown employee... Bob Jones, now Vice President of Communications for MJJ Productions. Bob Jones called me to express his sincere interest in my book, *Touched By The Jacksons*, which was about to be published, and wanted more detailed information about my project. Bob Jones, who has been working exclusively for Michael Jackson for years as his spokesperson, his publicist, his confidant, and his right-hand man, began his outstanding career some 40 years ago, writing a column for a small Black weekly newspaper so he could "get on the list." This quickly established him as a leading

THE REBIRTH

Public Relations (P.R.) representative and he acquired his first major celebrity campaign... working for the "Godfather of Soul" himself, James Brown. James Brown was making headlines during the Civil Rights movement of the 60's, leading the Black community into proclaiming "Say it loud, I'm Black and I'm proud!" Bob Jones was the man behind the man, the man behind the image, and the man behind the greatest Black entertainer of his time. With another notch added to his belt of success, Bob Jones sought work with the world's most prestigious Black record company... Motown Records. There Bob Jones' expertise in publicity flourished as he helped promote many of Motown's greatest performers, including the world famous Jackson Five. During the days of "Jackson-mania," Bob Jones was one of the driving forces behind the Jackson Five's worldwide success, which earned him even more recognition as a prominent P.R. agent.

As years went by, Michael Jackson took a risky step and branched away from his brothers, aspiring to achieve his own individual success as a solo artist. Remembering how Bob Jones was a great asset to him and his brothers years ago when they were with Motown, Michael recruited Bob again knowing that his P.R. expertise and talent was exactly what Michael was looking for. Michael Jackson has said of Bob Jones, that he is the epitome of competence, honesty, and loyalty and he's totally committed to excellence in his work. As Vice President of Michael's own MJJ Productions, his reputation supersedes him because Bob Jones is an unsurpassed icon in the field of Public Relations.

The abundance of God's blessings continued when I had the opportunity to meet the incomparable "Lady of Soul" herself, Ms. Gladys Knight. Her outstanding career began over 30 years ago, then known as the lead singer of the group, Gladys

Knight and the Pips, and their songs are a timeless treasure in music *history*. Gladys has defined the word "longevity" in her own right. She is pure success. And knowing that she was the first to bring the Jackson Five to Motown, it was a thrill to meet someone that played such an important role in the Jackson Five's careers.

    I received my first invitation as a special guest to Gladys Knight's performance at the MGM Grand Hotel and Casino in Las Vegas, Nevada, on March 15, 1998, by her manager, Mr. Jimmy Newman, who is also Gladys' son. Mr. Newman I commend for doing such a fantastic job with managing her astounding career, for her success is unparalleled. I was truly blessed to have finally met such a pure and wonderful, spirited soul that is *Gladys* at Harrah's Ak Chin Casino in Phoenix, Arizona on April 19, 1998. The one word that came to mind when she embraced me was "Love," and she represents the true meaning of the word. Gladys is like your sister, your best friend, and your mother all in one. And upon meeting her for the first time in the spring of 1998, I felt as though I had known her my entire life. She is a remarkable woman with a voice that evokes great emotion, raises your spirits, and stirs your soul. And I am humbly honored to have been blessed with the opportunity to meet the legendary Gladys Knight, for her name and her legend are everlasting, as she continues to play for sold-out venues around the world.

    My life was also enriched by a man whom I look up to and respect like a father figure because of all his personal experiences that he has shared with me and I have learned from. I met the man, Weldon Arthur McDougal III, through a mutual friend. I hadn't known my friend more than a few months, but he soon realized the potential friendship between Weldon and I, and put us in contact with one another. I spoke

THE REBIRTH

to Weldon over the phone for hours at a time, before we actually met in person. Weldon McDougal, a former Motown Records Promoter, representing some of Motown's top recording artists, including the world famous Jackson Five, also wrote a book about the infamous brothers that featured an extensive amount of rare photos from his personal collection, entitled *The Michael Jackson Scrapbook: The Early Days Of The Jackson Five.* Weldon not only worked with this young talented group, he also became a close friend of the Jackson family as well. Weldon confided in me many intimate details about the glory days of Motown, the Jackson Five, their careers, their personal lives, etc., and I felt honored that he had so much faith and trust in me as a friend.

When I finally visited Weldon at his home in Philadelphia for the first time, I was instantly awe-struck by the collection of celebrity photos that graced his walls. They were all candid shots of different celebrities like Diana Ross, Marvin Gaye, Bill Cosby, Gladys Knight, Smokey Robinson, The Temptations, Sammy Davis Jr., Mary Wilson, Billy Dee Williams, and of course, the Jackson Five. These were just some of the people who were either visiting him at his house, out on tour somewhere, in the studio, wherever. Weldon enjoyed taking photos of the famous Motown artists that he worked with, and other world renowned stars that he has encountered throughout his career, as is evident by the numerous photos that cover his walls. Like the photo he gave me of Michael Jackson, which is in my book, taken at Weldon's home, wearing a colorful, plaid top hat with the big fake flower on it. When I went to Weldon's home and saw that photo, I couldn't resist having Weldon take a picture of me wearing that very same hat, since he kept it in his collection all these years! Imagine—here I am at Weldon McDougal's house, posing for the photo of a lifetime, standing in the same room, wearing that very same hat Michael Jackson wore over 20 years ago! It was incredible!

One funny thing that Michael Jackson told Weldon when he was a kid, he said that when people from Philly talk, it always sounds like they're singing... they carry their words like they're carrying a note. I never gave it much thought until he told me that, but Michael's right. When I listen to Weldon speak, he doesn't say "hey man" he says *"hey maaann"* or *"allriiigghht."* He just kind of lets it *flow* when he speaks. He's a great man and since then we have formed a special bond of friendship that will always remain in spirit. Well you know the old saying, Philadelphia is the "City of Brotherly Love," and Weldon is the epitome of what that saying represents.

Another chapter in Michael's life enfolded with the rebirth of his soul. Michael Jackson decided it was time to share his heart and his life with a very special person and joined hands in marriage in May of 1994 with Lisa Marie Presley, daughter of the late, great Elvis Presley. Only *destiny* could bring together the King of Pop with the King of Rock 'N Roll's daughter and Michael has been royally blessed with the marriage of the century! The famous couple seemed inseparable as they made appearances all over the world hand-in-hand, in a display of marital bliss. They flaunted and taunted the press with their playful, fun-loving relationship, and the press ate it up like barracudas. Everyone wanted an exclusive interview, and only one person got the honors—Diane Sawyer for "Primetime."

I, like Michael Jackson, was also sought after for an exclusive interview with my wife... well, sort of. When "ABC World News Now" discovered that Michael and Lisa Marie were going to be interviewed by "Primetime" on June 14, 1995, they decided they wanted an exclusive interview of their own. I guess Michael and Lisa Marie turned them down, but they wanted an interview and they got an interview... with me as Michael Jackson and my wife Kristine as Lisa Marie. Since they couldn't get the royal couple to appear on their show, the producers decided to do a "spoof" interview of Michael and Lisa Marie, on the same night that they appeared on "Primetime," featuring the talents of me and my wife. I was honored that they chose me for the "interview" because they felt I was the closest to Michael Jackson that they could ever get. The only problem was, who would be their "Lisa Marie?" With a bit of quick thinking and visualization, I knew my wife would be the perfect candidate for the part, and they loved it! Can you believe that the real husband and wife, Michael and Lisa Marie were being portrayed by the other real husband and wife, Phoenix and Kristine! What a coincidence and a blessing it was for us to be the newlywed "Michael and Lisa Marie!" Kristine is not a professional actor or impersonator, but with some extra makeup, a brunette wig, and lights, camera, action, Kristine became Mrs. Lisa Marie Presley Jackson for the royal TV interview! We had a lot of fun shooting the segment for "ABC World News Now" in New York, and its sister stations across the country, the same evening following the real Michael and Lisa Marie interview with Diane Sawyer. We quickly took mental notes of "Primetime's" interview, and turned them into a hilarious skit, mimicking the King of Pop and his new bride. It was an experience that we both will always remember because it was a once in a lifetime opportunity—husband and wife played by husband and wife!

    But that wasn't the only television opportunity I had to portray Michael Jackson in a "spoof." "The Richard Bey Show" was also in need of a Michael Jackson for one of their Dating

Game segments, and called upon me to be "Michael Jackson." You may remember that Michael Jackson himself made an appearance on television's famed "Dating Game" show back in 1972 as the little celebrity guest bachelor looking for his first date. And now here I am 23 years later, in the summer of 1995, playing Michael Jackson on "The Richard Bey Show" in their "Dating Game" segment! The only difference was that I was on the panel of eligible bachelors instead of being the celebrity bachelor in search of a date. Who was the lucky winning bachelor on the show... of course it was "Michael Jackson!" From that one appearance on "The Richard Bey Show," filmed at the UPN 9 studios in Secaucus, New Jersey, I received so much notoriety and recognition that they called me back to appear in several more episodes.

Even though I loved performing as a Michael Jackson impersonator, and was successful in my career, I came to a fork in the road of my life and needed to do something for myself. I felt it was time for the world to know who "Phoenix" is, not who "Phoenix the Michael Jackson Impersonator" is. It was a great experience for me and it's been a long time coming, but a change had to come. I decided it was time to hang up my white glove and retire the black fedora. But I got a call to do one more show and it was an offer that I couldn't refuse! Hey, if I was going to officially retire, I wanted it to be an important, memorable event!

Joan Lunden, co-host of ABC-TV's "Good Morning America" in New York, had one of her assistants call my agent to hire me to make a special appearance at her daughter Lindsay's Bat Mitzvah celebration. I had previously met Ms. Lunden at a private affair in which I performed as Michael Jackson and she was very impressed with my stage performance. As she began planning for her daughter's 13th birthday celebration, I was a special guest on her list as a surprise for her daughter. I was honored to have had the opportunity to meet Joan Lunden and her family, who are all such gracious, wonderful people. Joan Lunden herself is such a beautiful woman on television, and even more exquisite in person. She's so stunning that from the moment you lay eyes on her, from a male's perspective, you become in awe of her radiant beauty. And my final Michael Jackson performance goes down in *history* for Ms. Joan Lunden at her daughter Lindsay's Bat Mitzvah in Tarrytown, NY on March 9, 1996.

Although I no longer perform as a Michael Jackson impersonator, one thing that I am proud to say about myself and my career as an impersonator, is that throughout my 15 years of performing as the world's greatest entertainer, *never ever* did I have any cosmetic surgery to make myself look more like Michael Jackson. I know there are many impersonators out there that have altered their features to obtain a closer resemblance to the King of Pop, but I'm proud to say that I've never had to rely on such drastic measures. These impersonators have gone too far with what they were doing and lost themselves in a persona that isn't even their own. They have tried to erase their facial features as though they were ashamed of who they are or where they come from, but at the same time, tried to look like someone else. They have tried to change their face to look like another person, someone very famous that already has that face and that hair, and they are no longer being true to themselves and who they are. Who do *they* see when they look at themselves in the mirror every day? At least I know when I look into the mirror I see myself and only myself, because once I take the makeup off I am *Phoenix* and no one else. I earned my success because of my talent, determination and hard work, not because of cosmetic surgery.

Other rebirths were happening in my life and Michael's life as well. Michael Jackson, the King of Pop, announced to the world the birth of his first son and heir to the Jackson throne, "Prince Michael," born on February 13, 1997. Little "Prince" was appropriately named after his great-grandfather Prince and father Michael. Michael Jackson and Lisa Marie Presley divorced in early 1996, and Michael then married his baby son's mother, Debbie Rowe, November 1996, in Sydney, Australia. It was a *tabloid junkie's* heaven for the media as Michael Jackson made headlines all over the world with his first marriage to Lisa Marie, their divorce two years later, his marriage to Debbie Rowe, and the birth of their son, Prince Michael. Michael was experiencing many changes in his life and I feel that the birth of his son Prince, sort of put Michael's life into a more positive perspective. For years, Michael gave so much of his time and his love to children around the world, but never did he have his own children to share his love with, until now. Not only has God blessed Michael with one angel, his son Prince Michael, God has also blessed him with a second angel, daughter Paris Michael Katherine, born April 3, 1998. With all the love that Michael has for all the children of the world, imagine just how much love he has for his two beautiful angels from Heaven. As a father myself, I know how much joy and love my children bring to my life every day, and I know how truly *happy* Michael is because of the love from his little Prince and Princess!

The newest re-birth in my own life came with the birth of my youngest son, TreyVon, on February 26, 1998. Little "Trey," whom I consider our "miracle baby," came into the world 6 weeks early but not a moment too soon. Even though he was born prematurely at 34 weeks, he was so healthy for his age and his size (4 lbs. 3 oz.), we knew what a blessing

THE REBIRTH

from God he truly is. Our little angel is one of the greatest blessings to our family—another *happy*, healthy baby boy. And I thank God every day for all He has done for me because I know deep in my heart that I am truly blessed with 5 strong, healthy, wonderful children.

While venturing down new paths of my life, I find inner peace and strength from God and my children. Although I have not seen my daughter Timanda since November 22, 1994, she is here with me, in my heart, in my soul, in every ounce of my life, in everything that I do. No matter where I go, no matter what I do, she is always with me, along with my four other children, for inspiration and encouragement. She may not be here with me now physically, but she is so close to me, I can feel her love and her angelic glow right beside me at all times. God knows I have never ever turned my back on my daughter, and my numerous court documents clearly demonstrate that. Her mother tried everything in her power to keep me from my daughter and finally succeeded by manipulating the system. She is to blame for the absence of a loving father in her daughter's life and will have to answer to God for her actions. My daughter is forever in my life and nothing will ever break the bond between us because *that's what love is made of*. And when the time comes for us to be together once again, she will find me. I have left many doors open for her to seek and find me, and have led the path for her to walk down to me. God will carry her and bring her to me, like in the "Footprints" poem, when she needs Him the most, He will be there for her. And *I'll be there*, too.

And the Jacksons will be there, as their music demonstrates their incomparable success around the world and their legendary fame. They serve as a reminder to us that as celebrities and superstars, they have endured... and as a family they have *triumph*ed. They have shown us what true family values are based on and that true family values are what kept them together when everyone, especially the media, were trying to tear them apart. Of course, no one is perfect, including the Jackson family, and they have admitted their imperfections, their troubles, and their mistakes. They have been true with themselves and true with the public, and for that I hold the utmost respect for them. In my eyes, they continue to be a role model family for children young and old to look up to because no matter what the circumstances, they have not let anyone or anything get between them as a family and proved that, as Jermaine stated, "blood is thicker than water."

Through my new journeys of life that God has set forth for me, I will continue to look up to the Jacksons for strength, encouragement, and inspiration. They have always been there for me as a spiritual reinforcement to follow my dreams, and as my dreams continue to become a reality, it is clear that my efforts have not been in vain. My life and my career have prospered beyond my expectations and it is all due to my own God given talents, my personal drive, and my faith. Jackie Jackson once shared these words of wisdom with me: "If you keep your heart pure, only good things can happen for you," and I will always live by those words. As I venture down new and unpaved roads in my life, I *keep the faith* that continues to lead me on the road to success and prosperity. And I know deep in my heart that it is my *destiny*, because I have been *touched by the Jacksons*.

THE REBIRTH

"Don't let no one get you down.
Keep moving on higher ground.
Keep fighting until
You are the King of the Hill.
No force of nature can break
My will to self-motivate.
They said my face that you see
Is destined for History!"

— ***Words spoken by a true man:***
Michael Jackson

From the author...

I would like to give special thanks to the following people:

- The Jacksons—Jackie, Marlon, Tito, Jermaine, Michael, and Randy, for inspiring me and touching my soul. *"2300 Jackson Street is always home."*

- Joseph and Katherine Jackson, for sharing your gifted family with the world.

- Berry Gordy and Motown Records, for presenting the Jackson Five to the world.

- Susanne dePasse, for opening the doors of Motown to the Jackson Five.

- Bobby Taylor from the Vancouvers, for bringing the Jackson Five to Motown.

- Diana Ross, for introducing the Jackson Five to the world.

- Gladys Knight, for discovering the Jackson Five. "You are a wonderful spirit."

- Hal Jackson, for letting the Jackson Five *do their thing* in 1969.

- Don Cornelius, for introducing so many new Black performers to the world and letting them take a ride on the Soul Train.

- The late, great Ed Sullivan, for giving the Jackson Five the first national television exposure.

- CBS/Epic Records, for giving the Jacksons the opportunity to produce beautiful music for all the world to enjoy.

- Bob Jones, for running, not walking, to the opportunity of a lifetime—working with the world's greatest entertainer, "The King of Pop," Michael Jackson.

- Quincy Jones, for setting records and making *history* with Michael Jackson.

- Smokey Robinson, my very dear friend, for writing a lifetime of beautiful songs that will last an eternity.

- Dick Clark, for opening up new doors for the Jackson Five.

- Cynthia Horner, for letting the Jackson Five be on the cover of the very first Black teen magazine, *Right On!*. Keep the dream alive!

- Frankie Crocker, for pushing the Jackson Five through the airwaves of Black radio.

- Weldon A. McDougal III, for sharing the wonderful days of Motown with me.

- Earl Bryant, my brother, for extending your hand in friendship and keeping it real.

- Tony Lewis, for your friendship and *brotherhood*.

FROM THE AUTHOR

- Eddie O'Jay, for inviting me into your "House of Blues."

- Steve Manning, for starting the very first Jackson Five Fan Club. *"We thank you for the joy."*

- All the fans, for believing and supporting the entire Jackson family from the past, present, and into the future.

- The Almighty God, for giving me five wonderful children, Timothy, Gemaile, Timanda, Frank, and Trey, and future "angels" that I may be blessed with. I love you all very much for making me the proudest and luckiest father in the world.

- My parents, Charles and Mary Phoenix, for bringing me and my siblings into the world... I love you.

- My dear and wonderful wife, Kristine, for her love and support and believing in me... *"I love your face."*

- The entire Phoenix clan, for encouraging me to follow my dreams... I love you all.

- Malka, for pulling together as parents and never breaking the chain

- Mrs. Barbara Hairston, for educating me not only in school, but spiritually through God.

- Reverend Richard Bell of Mt. Zion Baptist Church in Barnegat, New Jersey, for delivering your words of wisdom.

- My church family at Mt. Zion Baptist Church, for your love and prayers.

- Melissa Paul and family, for turning our friendship into a family.

- Angel and Dre, for their bravery, wisdom, and inspiration.

- The *Phoenix* Fan Club, for your love, support and dedication.

- My friends in Brooklyn (my hometown), you will always be in my heart.

- All my brothers at the Brooklyn House, "let not your mind and body be enslaved, but let your spirit and soul be free." *Keep the faith!*

If I have left anyone out of my VIP list, it was purely unintentional and my heart and spirit are always with you.

- **Special note** — To my daughter — *"Be Not Always"*

"*God is my Saviour, Salvation, and Keeper.*"

Phoenix

PHOENIX RISING

"ONE OF THE MOST BEAUTIFUL AND RARE CREATURES OF UNPARALLELED SPLENDOR IS THE MAGNIFICENT PHOENIX BIRD. THIS EXTRAORDINARY BIRD'S PLUMAGE DISPLAYS A RAINBOW OF GOLDEN IRIDESCENT COLORS THAT GLEAM FROM THE RADIANT SUNLIGHT. THIS AMAZING IMMORTAL CREATURE IS SAID TO BE BORN AND REBORN OF FIRE. THE PHOENIX BIRD INSTINCTIVELY FLIES TOWARDS THE SUN AND PERISHES ONLY TO RISE AGAIN FROM ITS OWN ASHES TO REGENERATE ITS LIFE ANEW.

I AM THE TRUE SPIRIT OF PHOENIX. IN MY LIFE, I HAVE FLOURISHED AND GOD HAS BLESSED ME FRUITFULLY. I HAVE SEEN AND EXPERIENCED SOME OF THE MOST WONDERFUL THINGS THAT LIFE HAS TO OFFER. BUT LIKE THE PHOENIX BIRD, I HAD TO SOAR INTO THE BURNING FLAMES FOR MY OWN RESURRECTION AND JUSTIFICATION. AT A PIVOTAL TIME IN MY LIFE, MY BODY AND FLESH WERE ENTRAPPED IN A TOMB WHICH WAS A MAZE WITHIN ITSELF. BUT MY SPIRIT FREED MY BODY AND SOUL FOR MY SALVATION AND I AM NOW WHOLE IN MY RENEWAL WITHIN GOD'S HOLY SANCTUARY OF ETERNAL EXISTENCE."

I AM PHOENIX.

POEM WRITTEN BY: PHOENIX

LYRIC COPYRIGHTS

Lyric excerpts from:

"We're Here To Entertain You" copyright 1976, written by Hal Davis, Nita Garfield, Charlotte O'Hara.

"The Dream Goes On" copyright 1992, written by Andy Anderson, Stephen Lunt, Eric Beall, Jermaine Jackson, John Barnes.

"Young Folks" copyright 1968, written by H. Gordy, A. Story.

"If'n I Was God" copyright 1972, written by Richard Sherman, Robert Sherman.

"Man In The Mirror" copyright 1987, written by Siedah Garrett, Glen Ballard.

"Off The Wall" copyright 1979, written by Rod Temperton.

"Be Not Always" copyright 1984, written by Michael Jackson and Marlon Jackson.

"Happy (Love Theme From "Lady Sings The Blues")" copyright 1972, written by William "Smokey" Robinson, Michael LeGrand.

"2300 Jackson Street" copyright 1989, written by Jermaine Jackson, Jackie Jackson, Tito Jackson, Randall Jackson, Gene Griffin, Aaron Hall.

"She's Good" copyright 1971, written by The Corporation.

"If You'd Only Believe" copyright 1989, written by Billie Hughes, Roxanne Seeman, Jermaine Jackson.

"Two Ships (In The Night)" copyright 1989, written by David Conley, Jermaine Jackson, Everette Collins.

"Tabloid Junkie" copyright 1995, written by Michael Jackson, James Harris III, Terry Lewis.

"Castles Of Sand" copyright 1978, written by M. McGloiry.

"They Don't Care About Us" copyright 1995, written by Michael Jackson.

"This Time Around" copyright 1995, written by Michael Jackson.

"HIStory" copyright 1995, written by Michael Jackson, James Harris III, Terry Lewis.

Opening dialogue from the Jacksons' 1984 Victory Tour, copyright 1984.

TOUCHED BY THE JACKSONS